WARTIME BATH
LIFE ON THE HOME FRONT 1939-45

DAVID AND JONATHAN FALCONER

IN MEMORY OF MY FATHER
David Falconer
19 April 1934 – 8 January 2002

© Jonathan Falconer 2022

Jonathan Falconer has asserted his right to be identified as the author of this work.

All rights reserved. No part of this publication may be reproduced or stored in a retrieval system or transmitted, in any form or by any means, electronic, mechanical, photocopying, recording or otherwise, without prior permission in writing from JJN Publishing.

First published in 2001 by Sutton Publishing as *Bath at War: The Home Front 1939-1945*.
This revised and updated new edition first published in 2022 by JJN Publishing Ltd.

British Library Cataloguing in Publication Data
A catalogue record for this book is available from the British Library.

Printed book 978 1 8384277 7 1
ebook 978 1 8384277 6 4

Published by JJN Publishing Ltd

www.jjnpublishing.com

Printed and bound in Malta

While every effort is taken to ensure the accuracy of the information given in this book, no liability can be accepted by the author or publisher for any errors in, or omissions from, the information given.

The author and publisher have taken all reasonable steps to identify the copyright status of the images reproduced in this book, but if anyone believes their copyright has been infringed, please contact the publisher.

CONTENTS

INTRODUCTION (2001 AND 2022) 08
1. PROLOGUE: 3 SEPTEMBER 1939 12
2. GEARING UP FOR WAR 16
3. THE WAR GETS UNDERWAY 36
4. BLITZ WEEKEND 50
5. BLITZ – THE AFTERMATH 88
6. BOMBER'S RETURN 116
7. FOOD, FUN AND CHEWING GUM 126
8. TOWARDS VICTORY 146
ACKNOWLEDGEMENTS 156
BIBLIOGRAPHY AND LIST OF SOURCES 157

QR CODES

We have added QR codes to certain photographs in this book. These link to Google Maps street view so you can see what the locations look like today. To use the QR codes you will need internet access and a smart phone or tablet. Simply point the camera on your device to scan the code and then click the link to view in Google Maps. This information was correct at the time of going to press.

INTRODUCTION (2001)

Almost a whole lifetime now separates us from the momentous events that are described in this book. At the time of writing, there can be few people living who remember clearly the details of everyday life in Bath during the Second World War.

After our first volume of *Bath at War* was published in March 1999, we soon realised there was a great deal more to be said about the experiences of Bathonians on the 'Home Front' during the last war. Our first book drew largely on editorial material from the *Bath Chronicle*, but judging from the letters and comments we received, we had merely scratched the surface. It became obvious that our next book should be based as much as possible on oral history interviews and previously unpublished contemporary letters and personal diaries – but where should we start to look?

The search for suitable source material was not always easy, and the response to our requests in local newspapers for personal recollections was on the whole disappointing. We quickly realised that a valuable fund of information lay much closer to home in the guise of our friends and acquaintances, of whom many have contributed to the accounts included here. Some of them initially thought that what they had to offer was of little significance. We leave our readers to judge that for themselves.

We are grateful to all those who so willingly agreed to write down their personal memories and to be interviewed. A specially devised

Frantic preparations are made to complete an air-raid shelter at Fairfield Park before war is declared. This one is to be used as an air-raid wardens' post. (*Bath Chronicle*)

INTRODUCTION

Bath on the eve of the Second World War, a city totally unprepared for (and unprotected against) attack from the air.

questionnaire often proved useful as a 'memory jog'. However, the vagaries of memory are such that recollections inevitably become elaborated and distorted with the passage of time. Everyday life during the war years, as described in books and depicted in films, has a tendency to lodge itself in the subconscious where it colours and blends with personal memories. Nevertheless, the testimonies of those now in their seventies and eighties, if treated cautiously, are of great value, and may be admitted to the canon of historical studies of the period.

Extracts from a number of previously unpublished personal letters are included in this book. The Matthews-Meem collection held at the Imperial War Museum in London is a series of wonderfully evocative letters written by a Bath GP, Dr Ted Matthews, to his evacuee daughters

The Assembly Rooms was hit by incendiaries in the third raid of the Blitz, early on Monday 27 April, which gutted the recently restored interior. Here, firemen damp down the still-burning fires during the Monday. The photograph was taken on Bennett Street. Note the Sedan Chair beside the railings, a relic from an earlier, but no less troubled, era.

in America. Extracts from this remarkable collection appear in print here for the very first time. Bath's medical fraternity must have been avid letter writers during the war years because we have been able to obtain an uncensored letter from another city GP, Dr Sammy Marle, written to his children in the aftermath of the Baedeker Blitz. This, too, is previously unpublished. (A fuller résumé of contributors and source material can be found elsewhere in the acknowledgements and bibliography.)

Because of the advancing years of our interviewees, we have been only too conscious of the need to place their memories on record. One of our elderly contributors, Grace Selley, was interviewed only a fortnight before she died in August 2000 aged 81. Although seriously ill at the time, Grace and her sister Eileen clearly enjoyed reliving their wartime experiences in Bath for the microphone, and it was a delight to hear them reminisce. Another sadness was the early death in September 2000 of Hylton Baynton-Coward at the age of 67.

We are aware that there must be people still living in Bath and the surrounding area whose lives have been scarred by personal tragedy as a result of the war. Nevertheless, we hope that these personal recollections of life on the Home Front in Bath will not only rekindle happier memories for some older Bathonians, and Bathonians by adoption, but also be of interest to people of younger generations who, thankfully, have not experienced the horrors of war at first hand.

David and Jonathan Falconer, 2001

INTRODUCTION (2022)

Soon after publication of the first edition of this book, my father David died unexpectedly after a short illness on 8 January 2002, aged 67. He was proud of his Bath roots and heritage and passionate about the history of his home city. During the course of our initial research, the process of speaking to others who had shared the experience of the Bath Blitz was cathartic for him. He had celebrated his eighth birthday on 19 April 1942, only a week before the raids, but even though he was a child the memories and feelings of those times, of being bombed in his home at Julian Road, stayed with him all his life.

Most of the people who spoke to us in the late 1990s about their wartime memories have since died. In 2022, the eightieth anniversary of the Bath Blitz, the war years have all but passed out of living memory and tangible links with those difficult times have almost gone. I was fortunate to speak with 95-year-old Sylvia Weeks (née Hancock) in October 2021 about her experience of the Blitz. As with my late father, Sylvia's recollections of the bombing had been imprinted on her memory and they were as clear today as they were 80 years ago.

In April 2008, I was invited to meet German former bomber pilot Willi Schludecker when he visited Bath to apologise for his part in bombing the city in 1942. My invitation was courtesy of Bath resident Chris Kilminster, who had lost members of his family in the Blitz, and whose friendship with Willi after the war had resulted in the latter's memorable visit. It was a morally challenging occasion for both men, which they embraced in the true spirit of reconciliation and, for Willi, of atonement. It was humbling to be present and witness this event.

In the 21 years that have passed since publication of the first edition of *Bath at War: The Home Front*, more information has become available, casting a fresh new light on many of the events described. Much of this has been made possible through improved access to public records and the publication online of reminiscences – both personally and by institutions like the Imperial War Museum. More photographs have also emerged, bringing a different focus to bear on the city during the war.

I hope this new edition of our book, published in the 80th anniversary year of the Bath Blitz, will introduce the story of Bath in the Second World War to a new audience – those who were either too young to catch it the first time around, or older readers who may have missed it when first published in 2001.

Jonathan Falconer, 2022

CHAPTER 1
PROLOGUE: 3 SEPTEMBER 1939

'... THIS COUNTRY IS AT WAR WITH GERMANY'

Those who remember Neville Chamberlain's broadcast on that fateful Sunday morning of 3 September 1939, can never forget its impact on them personally, and on the nation as a whole. When Chamberlain had arrived back in Britain the previous October from his summit with Hitler in Munich, his famous declaration of 'peace for our time' rang hollow and was greeted with scepticism. There were few people who believed that Hitler could be trusted.

For some time before the 3 September broadcast was made, the feverish diplomatic activity between London and Berlin had been followed avidly in the press and on the wireless by millions of Britons. They hoped against hope that war could be averted – even at the eleventh hour. Eileen Rogers, who lived in Englishcombe Lane and who had just left Oldfield Girls' School, recalls, 'during that time we all thought we were going to be at war'. People generally were pessimistic about a satisfactory diplomatic solution.

On 1 September came the news that German forces had invaded Poland, a country with which Britain had a treaty. Further diplomatic activity followed, but to no avail. Hitler refused to withdraw his troops. And so, on Sunday 3 September, families up and down the country waited anxiously by their wireless sets for the inevitable announcement that Britain was at war. David Falconer has hazy memories of the outbreak of war: 'We used to go on a fortnight's summer holiday to Weymouth where we all stayed at Sydney Hall. Daily excursions were made to Weymouth beach and to the beach at Portland. I remember sitting with my mother near Portland lighthouse and seeing a submarine surface not far off the coast. To a small boy of five-and-a-half it was a frightening experience. We were at Weymouth when war broke out and I can dimly recall sensing the mood of anxiety among the adult members of our party as preparations were made for an early return to Bath.' That Sunday morning, eleven-year-old 'Tim' Cuppage and her mother went as usual to the Abbey for the 11 o'clock service of Matins. In common with the rest of the congregation they were

David Falconer on the beach at Weymouth in August 1939. With the threat of war he and his family returned home to Bath.

PROLOGUE: 3 SEPTEMBER 1939

A face made for tragedy. The Prime Minister, Neville Chamberlain, speaks to the nation on 3 September 1939.

mildly surprised when the Rector, Archdeacon Marshall Selwyn, mounted the stairs to the pulpit and placed a small wireless set in front of the microphone. The initiative for this unexpected action seems to have come from Mrs Jackman who, earlier in the day, had telephoned the Rector and suggested that her son Aubrey should bring his portable wireless set to church so that the congregation would not miss the premier's broadcast.

At 11 o'clock the silent and anxious congregation awaited the dreaded announcement. Fifteen minutes later they heard Chamberlain's familiar voice come on the air to tell the nation that although Britain had called for Hitler to withdraw his troops from Poland, 'no such undertaking has been received and that, consequently, this country is at war with Germany'.

'Tim' has 'no definite memories of emotions experienced at that moment, except an awareness that our safe, secure, ordered lives were about to change'. At this distance of time, one can only imagine the thoughts and feelings of those in the congregation, both young and old, as the service continued after the broadcast. A young Aubrey Jackman, one of the sidesmen, remembers thinking to himself as he took the collection, 'It's all right for you old geezers, I shall certainly become a soldier and not live to see the end of the war.'

Phyllis Bond remembers waiting by the wireless set at her home in Albany Road, Twerton, for 'that dry-as-dust voice to say "we are at war with Germany". I was 19 years old and engaged to be married and I set off to meet my fiancé, and he'd had the same idea and we met each other halfway. We knew, of course, that he would be called up. He was 24 years old and working in a shop – not a reserved occupation.'

Across town, at the end of the Paragon and opposite Hedgemead Park, Grace Wiggins and her sister Eileen were attending the morning service at Walcot church where Grace's banns of marriage were to be called for the third time. Grace recalled: 'this old chap – the verger, I think – came into church to say that war had been declared. I shall never forget it! I felt dreadful about it. I was 21 at the time.'

Britons had been shown how to use gas masks when the Munich Crisis blew up in 1938, but with the outbreak of the Second World War a year later these instructions were at last for real.

Nineteen-year-old Hester Chivers (known to family and friends as Lita) was living in a flat at 11 Kingsmead Street with her parents James and Mary and brother Edwin. She remembers there had been talk and rumours about the possibility of war. 'When it came over the radio on that Sunday morning, my mother and I sat and cried. It didn't seem possible that it should come after all the politicians had done to avoid it. It seemed that the end of the world had come.'

Dr Ted Matthews, a Newbridge GP, writing from Bath on the same day, began his letter:

'So the storm has burst. Today has been a day of hectic preparations even in this safe spot. Between blacking out windows – which in the cold weather rather makes the house like an oven – we have rushed to the wireless for every news bulletin. Thank God we have had the strength of mind to stand up to

PROLOGUE: 3 SEPTEMBER 1939

 Schoolgirls from Walcot troop along the London Road at Kensington on an outing in 1939. Their 'crocodile' is preceded by a party carrying gas masks in a laundry basket.

the Nazi system at last. I think the relief of knowing something definite, of realising that we have kept faith with Poland, far outweighs the shock of plunging into the ghastly business of war.'

Pamela Taylor was living with her father and stepmother at 'Melville' in Milton Avenue, when she heard about the declaration of war. She was 13 years old: 'We had been to church at Beechen Cliff and we came home and dad put the wireless on and we heard Neville Chamberlain talking. I got excited because some friends had told me we would all be evacuated, and I thought this would be lovely. My dad was really upset because he had been in the Great War as a lieutenant in the Gloucesters and had been very badly wounded on the Somme. Mum wasn't quite so much worried, even though she had been through the Great War, too.'

On the same day, Eileen Rogers and her family, especially her father, were glued to the radio once they knew war was imminent:

'News of the outbreak of war came over the radio and the first thing we had to do was go over to the Englishcombe Inn and have our gas-masks issued and fitted, and that was our very first introduction, and then we realised we were at war. My sister-in-law had a baby who had to go inside one of those big infant masks. For the rest of the day I wondered if the sirens were going to go. Nothing did happen, of course.'

And nothing of any note did happen for some considerable time – the period from the declaration of war until the early summer of 1940 became known in Britain as the 'bore' war and the 'phoney' war. Preparations for war begun some years earlier continued to be made, but now with a much greater sense of urgency.

CHAPTER 2
GEARING UP FOR WAR

With the outbreak of hostilities, the niceties of prewar Britain came to an abrupt end and a way of life changed forever. In common with every other town and city across the land, Bath felt the impact with the immediate introduction of the 'blackout' and the mobilisation of the Auxiliary Fire Service (AFS). During the next two days local Air Raid Precautions (ARP) schemes swung into operation – first aid posts and ambulance depots were established, and rescue parties and decontamination units were formed. Air raid wardens' posts began to function and were manned full-time.

In common with many other young people, Eric Lanning, just out of school, was keen to 'do his bit': 'A few days before the outbreak of war, the citizens of Bath were asked to help fill, and put in place, sandbags around the Guildhall. Both my brothers and I volunteered for this task, and I recall building a wall of sandbags on the pavement in front of the main entrance.'

'Tim' Cuppage, an only child, lived with her parents at 20-21 Victoria Terrace on the Lower Bristol Road where her father, Dr Burke Cuppage, was in practice as a GP. Theirs was a working-class area. She recalls:

> 'We were the only professional family in the community. Our social life was spent among the medical fraternity and others of similar background. However, we were totally accepted by, and comfortable with, all our neighbours and local shopkeepers, many of whom were patients of my father's practice. It was a law-abiding community where people respected each other, and many elderly relatives were integral to the households. The notion of class was very marked, not just between upper, middle and lower, but there was a hierarchy accepted then, between, for example, the waterworks operator and the coalmen, both living in our road. There was continuity of occupancy, both of homes and shops: the post office, butcher, dairy, pickle factory, laundry, the Keevil brothers' workshop, Mr Amos the cobbler in Brougham Hayes, the fish and chip shop at the end of Victoria Buildings, and Mr Hudd the newsagent at the other end.'

Before the war, and for some time later, Dr and Mrs Cuppage employed

GEARING UP FOR WAR

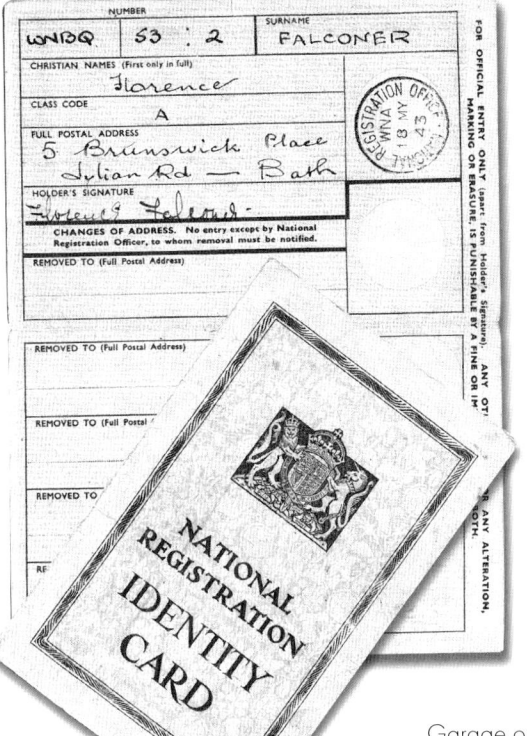

National Registration Identity Cards had to be carried by everyone. They were issued to newborn babies within two weeks of their birth. This card belonged to the authors' mother and grandmother.

a cook and a parlourmaid, but once the war proper began they left. 'Amelia the cook didn't like the peripheral effects of the Bristol Blitz and went home to Oakhill, and the parlourmaid became a landgirl.'

For some time before the war, older men had been expected to join the Territorial Army (the 'Terriers') or the Auxiliary Fire Service. Ray Burgess and some of his friends joined 17 Division of the AFS. He was based at Cleveland Bridge, at that time both a fire and an ambulance station, where he was employed in the workshop. ''When vehicles broke down, you went out and got them.' Gradually, after war broke out, some of the younger firemen were called up for active service in the armed forces. Once the war had started, Ray and his colleagues had to go out to buy cars for towing trailer pumps, and the cars had to be fitted with towing brackets. Brown's Garage on the Bear Flat, and Steele's on the Lower Bristol Road were commandeered and converted for use as fire stations.

'One thing that stands out in my memory is going to Englishcombe Farm, I think it was called. They [the AFS] had taken over some of it and one of the vehicles wouldn't start, so they sent for me to do something about it. I said to one of the chaps, "what's the smell?" He said, "It's the bull next door." And in the yard next door there was a bull up to its knees in muck!'

Once the war had started, new words and phrases began to enter people's everyday vocabularies: 'billetees', 'vackies' (evacuees), 'utility', 'coupons', 'call-up', 'black-out', 'wardens', 'black-market', 'under-the-counter', 'requisitioning', 'all-clear' and so on. Ration books containing coupons for various foodstuffs were issued to everybody, and National Identity Cards had to be carried by all. Even babies were not exempt – identity cards were issued to them within a few weeks of their birth. As the war progressed, clothing and furniture were rationed. Both were manufactured to a specified 'utility' standard and bore a special sign of two round 'cheeses' with slices taken out of them.

 Great Pulteney Street as seen from Laura Place during the war. The Pulteney Hotel (at the left of the picture with flag flying) was one of a number of Bath hotels and other buildings requisitioned by the Admiralty at the outbreak war for use as office accommodation. Prior to this, for over 60 years the hotel had been owned by the Jackman family.

Within hours of the outbreak of war, Government contingency plans were dusted down and set in motion. Among these was the compulsory requisitioning of materials, equipment and buildings – indeed, anything and everything could be requisitioned by the Government to meet the demands of the war effort.

Plans for the evacuation of certain Government departments from London to the provinces had been laid well in advance of the anticipated outbreak of hostilities. Eric Lee, an Admiralty draughtsman working in Whitehall, came down to Bath with his department soon after the outbreak of war:

> 'The heads of departments and branches were given sealed orders, which were to be opened only when they were instructed to do so. The time came when the staff were told to pack essential records in boxes, which, in the case of Naval Construction Department, had to be marked "AA2, DNC, Section No.?". We learned later that "AA" stood for Bath and the "2" for the Grand Pump Room Hotel.'

Among the prominent buildings in Bath to be immediately requisitioned by the Government for use by the Admiralty were the larger hotels in the city centre. Aubrey Jackman's family had owned the Pulteney Hotel in Laura Place for over 60 years:

GEARING UP FOR WAR

'It had been my home for the first 18 years of my life, but now we were out in 35 hours. My father's quite famous collection of pictures (there were 3,017 on the inventory), beautiful classic antique furniture, curtains, lighting chandeliers, beds and linen were all loaded on to open lorries and driven into the depths of Somerset to be stored at Butleigh Castle. My mother and I moved to the Lansdown Grove Hotel, which my family also owned.'

Eileen Rogers remembers, as early as the Friday before war was declared, the indecent haste with which the Empire Hotel cleared out all its residents: 'They were mostly well-to-do people. They had to leave quickly, and all their suitcases and trunks were outside on the pavement, and there were taxis rolling up for them. They were just taken to wherever they could go, and the Admiralty came in more or less straight away on that Friday. As they moved out, so they almost moved right in.'

Eric Lee's arrival in Bath was memorable for several reasons:

'As the train from Paddington drew into the station we were greeted with the cries of "Baa, baa. Baa, baa", later understood to be Bath Spa, Bath Spa. We were lucky to have travelled in the front of the train and to have alighted on the platform and not on the parapet of the bridge over the Avon, which we would have done had we travelled in the rear. There were many volunteers with their private cars to take us to the various addresses. Mr W.H. Foster, the General Secretary of the YMCA, gave us a warm welcome and provided us with an excellent meal at 5.00pm – our first meal since an early breakfast in London.'

Eileen Rogers (later Rosevear) pictured (right) with her sister in the summer of 1940 outside their home at Englishcombe Lane.
(Paul Rosevear)

Frank Mawer, then an 18-year-old Admiralty clerk in London, came down to Bath by train on 24 September:

'All we were told was, "Be at Paddington at 9 o'clock and jump on the train". On the train, seats had been reserved for various Admiralty departments. Eventually we arrived at Bath, and that's where we were told to get off. We'd never seen it ... it looked a most beautiful place. We were told that our billets were laid on, largely for the department I was in, on the Bristol side of Bath – the Newbridge area,

Rudmore Park, actually. Mrs Gray, the dear lady who looked after me, really did it very well. She was very conscientious about things.'

At the beginning of the war accommodation in the city was at a premium, not only because of the influx of Admiralty personnel, but also because of the large number of people who had been evacuated from London and other British cities where there was the threat of bombing. Bath residents with room to spare in their houses and flats were obliged to take these people as 'billetees', and the Admiralty billettees came to be known as 'guinea pigs'.

Joan Barlow was among younger Admiralty women who were sent down from London; she also came towards the end of September and found herself working at offices set up in the former Pulteney Hotel:

'We became known locally as "guinea pigs", as Bathonians were obliged to accommodate us with bed, breakfast and one main meal a day for which they were paid one guinea [21s = £1.10] per person per week. We had one guinea deducted from our pay, which initially left me with seven shillings per week. This sum remained unaltered for the duration of the war and for householders it became a bone of contention with the city's billeting authorities.

'I had three different billets. The first near Sham Castle lasted two weeks and was with an elderly couple with an Austrian servant who clearly did not want the extra work. There were "DO NOT ..." notices everywhere. Eventually I went to a hostel for ladies only – a large house in its own grounds in Weston Park. The lounge was beautifully furnished with a baby grand piano. Most of the other rooms were turned into bedrooms. Here we were lucky and given our own rations of butter and sugar (small quantities, of course). All the baths had a line drawn at five inches, which everyone was asked not to exceed. Who the owners of the house were, I do not know, it is no longer in existence.'

Another young member of the Admiralty staff who came down from London on 20 September was Ivor Barnsdale, who was billeted in Oldfield Park. He had received his call-up papers but was prevented from enlisting in the armed services, or even joining the Home Guard, because of the nature of his work with the Admiralty. His future wife was evacuated from the West London suburb of Kew to Bath where she worked in the Employment Exchange in James Street West, paying out benefit money to civilian evacuees. Her father was also evacuated to Bath with the Admiralty.

Trevor Canham in the uniform of a lieutenant in the Royal Navy Volunteer Reserve. He trained as an observer and served in the Fleet Air Arm with 836 Naval Air Squadron flying Swordfish biplanes from the MAC carrier *Empire McAlpine* on Atlantic convoy escort duties. (*Trevor Canham via Pat Woods*)

Trevor Canham, then aged 17, had arrived in Bath in late July 1939 to take up a post as a junior 'worker-up' with the quantity surveyors W.E. Underwood & Sons, whose premises were at 1 Northumberland Buildings. He lived in lodgings near the bottom of Widcombe Hill. After meeting Cecil Cocks, the two young men started a Wolf Cub pack at the Congregational Church in Argyle Street in 1941. Cecil joined up later that year and Trevor moved into Cecil's parents' flat at 29 Pulteney Street. At evening classes, Trevor met John Glover, who was then with the Admiralty architects' department. It was John who invited Trevor to join the Abbey Youth Fellowship. He then found himself with other members of the fellowship's Abbey fire-watching team on duty on Wednesday nights.

Other factors had affected the billeting situation in the city. Bath had already suffered two waves of temporary residents – Irish labourers and London schoolchildren. The former were employed in building huge underground ammunition dumps in quarries at Corsham and Monkton Farleigh. Eric Lee remembers that 'they rather enjoyed themselves on the town at weekends and soon received a bad reputation'. However, they were later to redeem themselves in the eyes of Bathonians by their acts of bravery and sheer hard work in the aftermath of the Bath Blitz in 1942. As for the London schoolchildren, many had never seen apples growing on trees before. Eric Lee again:

> 'They showed the local boys how to steal them. Inevitably, the London boys usually escaped capture, but the local boys were not so lucky. The London boys also created havoc in their targeting of the horse chestnut. Disregarding the traffic, which was negligible in comparison with that of the metropolis, they wandered freely for the capture of the coveted conker.'

As we have seen, the Government had the power to requisition virtually anything, and it was not long before historic iron railings and gates in Bath were removed as 'scrap' to be turned into bombs and bullets. Among the early casualties of the drive for scrap iron were the historic Crimean War cannons in the Victoria Park, displayed close to the Victoria obelisk. The only railings untouched were those enclosing the 'areas' of basements. They were spared for obvious safety reasons.

> At 'Tim' Cuppage's house in Victoria Buildings on the Lower Bristol Road, the front garden was bordered by iron railings, which were removed to be melted down; some of the stumps still remain. In fact, stumps of railings can still be seen in many places in the city. Margo Cogswell remembers 'coming up over Bear Flat to see all the railings being taken away. I was absolutely aghast. They told me they were

taking them away to be made into bombs and ammunition, but I believe many of them were not used.'

Grace Wiggins was married to Victor Selley at Walcot church on 11 September 1939. After their marriage they were in the fortunate position of having their own house on Combe Down, and they took in a couple from London who had come down to work at the Admiralty. Many lasting friendships were forged between Bath residents and their billetees. 'Tim' Cuppage remembers that they had a 'vackie', a girl from London, 'possibly through a children's society'. She lived with them for some time and went to school locally. But Mrs Cuppage didn't find the arrangement easy.

Eileen Rogers, then living at Englishcombe Lane, remembers that, in the first months of the war:

'Along our road there were several evacuee children billeted. We didn't have any in our house because we were a big family and full up. Others had Admiralty staff billeted with them and therefore couldn't take any evacuees either. So your homes were open, really, to any and everybody who needed to come and work in Bath, and for children evacuated from the air raids. It was quite amusing because we soon realised they had different accents to us, London accents, but they went to school with us. I was quite friendly with two of them living next door but one to us. I think they were brought around in taxis and taken to church halls where people met them and took them home from there.'

In the years leading up to the Second World War, Jews desperate to escape Nazi persecution in Germany, Austria and Czechoslovakia found the world's doors of refuge closed – except in Great Britain. Late in 1938, the British Government agreed to accept 10,000 children, mostly Jewish, but the Nazis insisted on three conditions: the sum of £50 per child had to be paid, all children had to be aged between 2 and 17, and they had to flee alone – that is, without their parents or families.

Many organisations and individuals assisted in settling these children, as well as with offers of foster homes and houses for possible group homes. Lists of children were forwarded to London for selection and the numbers were ultimately determined by the practicalities of transportation and whether a sponsor could be found. These children of the Kindertransport (Children's Transport), as it was named, were dispersed to many parts of the British Isles and some came to Bath.

Bath High School resolved to admit Jewish refugee children under a scholarship scheme established by its governing body, the Girls' Public

Eva Ursula Krambach was born in Leipzig, Germany in 1924. Her parents Peter and Johanna sent her to England on the Kindertransport in March 1939. She joined Bath High School and spent some of her leisure time with the Fussell family at their home at Southfield House, Rode. Eva sailed to Canada on 17 October 1943, where she was reunited with her parents. She eventually settled in Staten Island, New York, where she married and raised a family. Eva died in 2017, aged 92.

Day School Trust, and by 1940 at least three refugee girls had joined the High School on Lansdown Road. In her book *Bath High School 1875–1998*, author Mary Ede recalls that one of the Kindertransport girls stood out from the crowd:

'[She] was remembered for her solo singing of Stille Nacht at the end of term assembly: Eva Krambach was about 14 when she came to England from Germany in March 1939. She was sponsored by Miss Corbett, one of the local committee, and boarded at Beaumont. She spent holidays with the Fussell family at Rode and then lived with them until she was able to join relatives in the USA.'

Bob White, a pupil at City of Bath Boys' School at the outbreak of war, remembers:

'I was in the second or third year and we had two German Jews who were evacuated. One of them was brilliant, he could speak English better than we could, do anything better than we could – he just put us in the shade. I often wonder what happened to him. His name was Littour, I think. The other one, I don't think he was a German, wasn't as brilliant as the other one and was a bit of a lad.'

This Civil Defence poster, painted by the artist Jack Matthew in 1939, encouraged women to volunteer for the Government's Evacuation Service.

Mary James and her family had one evacuee child billeted with them at King Edward Road. Mary was friendly with another girl, Dorli Kessler, who was billeted with a family in nearby Hensley Road. She was in the same year at school as Mary. And there was also a Polish girl aged about 13 or 14 who didn't stay very long, it was believed that for some reason she was interned.

About a quarter of Kindertransport children emigrated to the USA after the war and, like their contemporaries who remained in England, they survived the Holocaust. But more than 1.5 million of their peers could not be saved and died in Hitler's death camps.

The number of evacuee children being admitted to the City of Bath Girls' School early in the war became the cause of some concern to the headmistress, Miss Thatcher. Her speech at the annual prize giving on 13 November 1940 revealed why:

'In one respect at least, we are taking our share of the difficulties due to the Evacuation. Not only do our numbers continue to grow unceasingly, but we have to contend with the constant passage through the school of girls who stay only for a short period. Between September 1939 and July 1940, out of 204 girls admitted, 70 left after periods varying from a few weeks to a few months.

'The September invasion threat followed by the bombing of London caused something like a repetition of last year's experience. Already this term, 138 new pupils have been admitted, making a total of 343 entrants since the war began, more than the total population of the school in previous years.'

Margo Cogswell and her family at Hensley Road took in two billetees. One was Marjory, an Australian, and the other, Sally, a Londoner. Both women had been evacuated to Bath with Marks & Spencer's accounts department from London because of the likelihood of bombing; they worked at offices in Westgate Buildings opposite the Co-op.

Ray and Audrey Burgess had a girl named Pamela from London in their home at 48 Faulkland Road, but she stayed only a few months. Audrey remembers:

'She came up to South Twerton School with me. Her parents used to come and visit her at weekends on a Sunday. When my mum laid the table for our tea and she asked Pamela if she'd like an egg, she asked what that was. And she didn't sit at the table. We had to put the chair in and tell her to sit there. She didn't really cope with knives and forks. She was more accustomed to using her fingers. We felt sorry for her in a way, she didn't really make friends with anyone. After it died down she went back to London. None of the evacuees were very well behaved. The lady next door had two little girls and they were just of the same breed. I don't know how they had been brought up.'

Wyndham Paisey from Rose Hill Terrace in Larkhall was away serving with the RAF at St Athan in South Wales. He wrote to his fiancée Vera in Batheaston on 14 September 1940, voicing concerns about the influx of evacuees to the city:

'You say there are hundreds of evacuees come to Bath again. It will be a bit of a nuisance if Mum has to take them in again won't it? It wouldn't be so bad if they were clean, decent children. We like to feel we are helping them, seeing that so many of them are homeless now, but when they are so cheeking it's a different matter isn't it and, as you say, it certainly will be a bit of a bother for when I come home on weekends.'

For many children evacuated from some of the poorer areas of London, the experience of improved living conditions made its mark on them. The Chivers family took in two little boys at their flat in Kingsmead Street. 'It was an experience,' recalls Lita Chivers. 'They were aged seven and nine and came from Bethnal Green. They were with us for a long time until their parents decided to have them home when there was a lull in the bombing. They did not want to go – they found our home better than their own.'

Pamela Taylor's parents took in a billetee at Milton Avenue:

Wyndham Paisey, whose family lived at Larkhall, was concerned by the unruly behaviour of some evacuated children. (*Rose Scriven*)

'When the young girl arrived I was scared stiff. She wet the bed so much that mum had to get rid of her. She was about ten and from London. She was a real little * * * * *. She went to school at St Mark's. She wasn't a bad kid, but mum couldn't put up with her. Then mum took the Admiralty people – billetees. We had two men who were very nice. We had them until of course the house was bombed. Luckily, they were away when it happened.'

As far as Brian Hamilton was concerned, the arrival of the evacuees at Bathampton changed their village school 'beyond recognition':

'Initially there was some tension, but they soon fitted in. Occasionally we would play jokes on the parents when they came to visit, telling them that the cows were bulls and quite dangerous. To see them running when they were having a picnic was stupid, but to us children it appeared quite funny. However, we became quite friendly with many of them, and were delighted when some of them revisited the village years later.'

Evacuation was not just confined to the inhabitants of major cities and refugees from Europe. Fearful of a German invasion of Britain, some parents with young children decided it would be safer to send their offspring overseas to the comparative safety of the Dominions and the United States, where they would be billeted for the duration with host families. Through the British Government's Children's Overseas

Resettlement Scheme, 1,530 children were sent to Canada, 577 to Australia, 353 to South Africa, 202 to New Zealand, and another 838 children were sent to the USA by the American Committee in London.

Dr Ted Matthews, a GP, who lived with his wife and five children at 63 Newbridge Hill, decided soon after the outbreak of war to send his four eldest daughters across the Atlantic to the USA. He and his wife were concerned for the psychological well-being of their girls should they be forced to live under a repressive Nazi regime in Britain. In August 1940, the Matthews sisters embarked from Glasgow to Canada on the 20,000-ton liner SS *Duchess of York*, their destination being the home of the Meem family in Santa Fé, New Mexico – in more than one sense a world away from 'old worlds' Bath. On 23 August the Matthews received a telegram: 'Your lovely girls arrived safely. Will guard and cherish them. John Meem.' They eventually returned to England in August 1944. As for the SS *Duchess of York*, she was destined not to survive the war: the liner was set on fire and sunk by German bombers off the coast of Portugal on 11 July 1943.

Dr Ted Matthews (centre) in festive mood poses for the camera at a wartime Christmas fancy dress party at St Martin's Hospital. (*Bridget Wakefield*)

In a letter written in mid-September to the eldest Matthew daughter, Judy, from her school friend, Jean Mann, at Bath High School, concerns were expressed for her safety when it became known that a British passenger liner carrying evacuee children had gone down in the Atlantic:

> 'I expect you heard about the ship being sunk? Well, when I got to school in the morning several of the form were already there and they almost shouted at me "was Judy on the ship?" They were relieved when I told them that you were safely at your destination. One or two had caught early buses to find out from me quicker.'

The ill-fated vessel was the *City of Benares*, an 11,000-ton passenger liner carrying some 400 passengers and crew, and 90 evacuee children on their way to a new life in Canada. On 17 September 1940, when 600 miles and four days out from Liverpool, the liner was torpedoed by the German U-boat, U-48. The *City of Benares* sank with the loss of 258 lives including 77 of the children on board. This tragedy effectively put an end to the resettlement scheme.

GEARING UP FOR WAR

Blackout regulations had been imposed three days before the declaration of war. The windows (and doors if necessary) of every building had to be fitted with blackout material of some kind – thick curtains, cardboard, and other similar materials readily available in the shops. Lita Chivers recalls how 'it was a ritual, once it became dark, to pull the black curtains'. Street lighting was not allowed, and the lights of all motor vehicles had to be fitted with special masks so that only a limited amount of light shone on the road. In towns and cities the speed limit was reduced to 20mph. Kerbstones and lamp-posts were painted white to aid motorists in the blackout.

On arriving at Bath Spa station, Admiralty draughtsman Eric Lee has a clear recollection of the efficacy of the precautions. 'The blackout was perfect and we groped our way, enquiring for directions as we went, to the Grand Pump Room Hotel. We learned from this little walk in the darkness that no two kerbstones in Bath were of the same height.'

Mary James, whose father owned a pharmacy in Shaftesbury Road, remembers that: 'You daren't show a light, and going out of doors was pretty tricky. In the shop we had an old blanket across the door. Fortunately, it was a double door and fairly narrow and one side could be

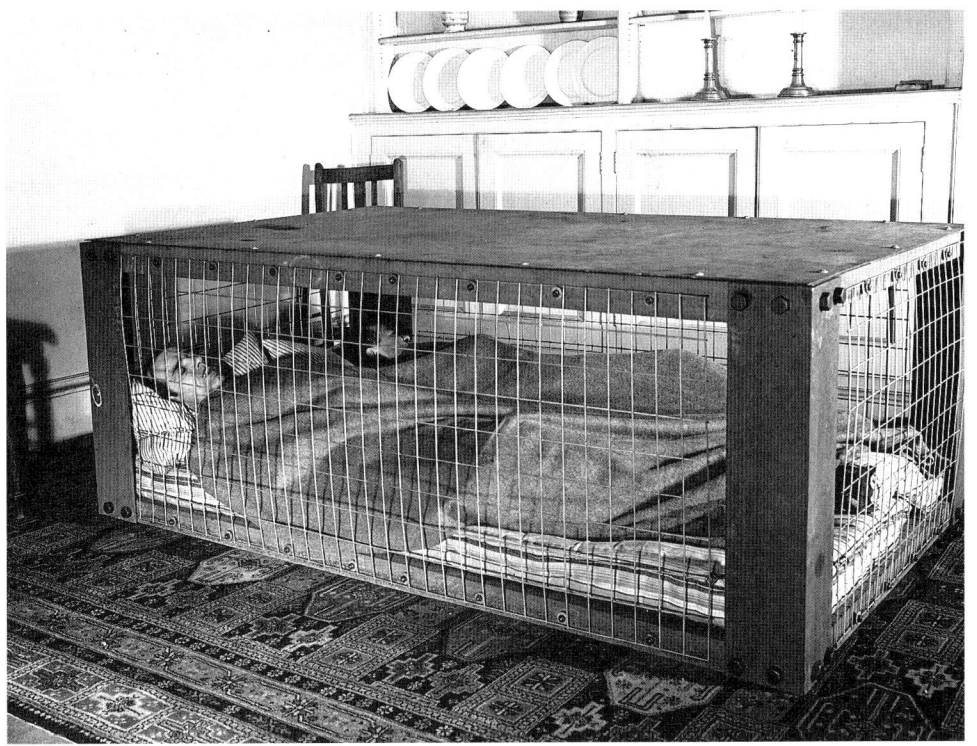

The indoor Morrison shelter, named after the government minister in charge of air-raid precautions, Herbert Morrison. The wire mesh could be removed so that the frame could form a table.

opened. So long as the light didn't shine out of the door we were alright.'

The issue of gas masks to young and old soon got under way. Betty Cottle's younger sister, Pat, the baby of the family '... had to be put right inside the gas mask. It was like a spacesuit and it had this pump on the side. The Mickey Mouse masks were the coloured ones they used to give the young children. Everywhere we went ... we had to take these gas masks. We were always buying new cases for them.'

Mary James remembers being fitted for her gas mask 'over the Co-op in Moorland Road. We went in a back entrance.' Brian Hamilton's father, being the senior ARP warden at Bathampton, had the job of organising the distribution of gas masks in the village. 'Many people had difficulty in fitting them. I was used at first as a demonstrator. Later it was found that I was able to persuade the old ladies and the children to wear the masks and keep them with them at all times.'

Sometime before the outbreak of war, plans were made to provide every household with an air raid shelter in areas expected to be vulnerable to air attack. There were two types of shelter: the outdoor, tunnel-shaped steel 'Anderson', named after Sir John Anderson, who was Minister of Home Security before the war, and later the indoor 'Morrison' shelter, named after Herbert Morrison who succeeded Anderson as minister in charge of air raid precautions in October 1939. Writing in May 1942, Dr Ted Matthews at Newbridge Hill noted:

> 'The Morrison shelter – which is given away to anyone who can't afford to buy one – is like a large, solid dining room table made of steel. There is room for four people or more underneath it and it has a sort of wire mattress on which they can make a bed. It must be made of astonishing stuff because over and over again a whole house has fallen on top of it and the people underneath have escaped without a scratch.'

Christina Brooks' family had a Morrison shelter, erected in their dining room, that they also used as the table for the duration of the war. 'My mother left supplies of sweets and drinks and some other essentials in the shelter with books for me and my brother, a torch, some candles and matches, and blankets and warm clothes.'

In the cellar at Victoria Buildings the Cuppages had a Morrison shelter 'that had been cleaned, cleaned, and whitewashed, and we had camp beds down there'. Eileen Rogers recalls that they were 'huge great things. They had to be constructed because you couldn't lift them yourself. When the sirens went we used to get in there. We had an old mattress inside the

GEARING UP FOR WAR

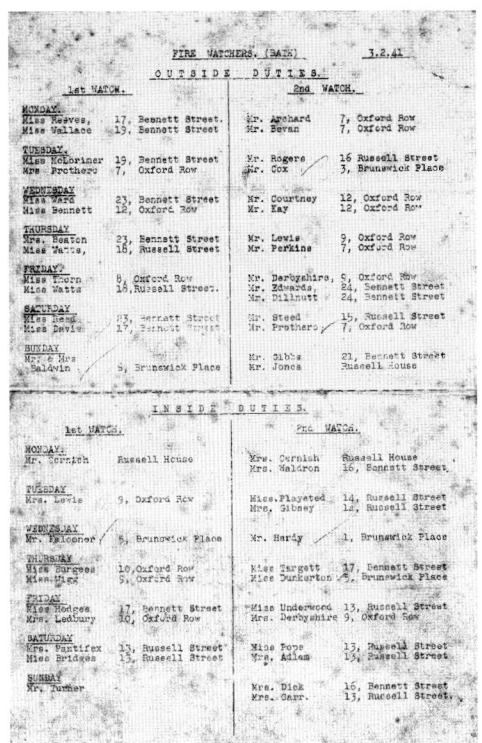

This fire watchers' roster for 3 February 1941 covers an area of duty bounded by Bennett Street, Russell Street, Brunswick Place and Oxford Row on Lansdown Road. It is divided into two watches covering outdoor and indoor duties, each with two watches. It would have been an arrangement that was replicated in neighbourhoods across the city. The authors' father and grandfather was on inside duty in the first watch at 5 Brunswick Place.

shelter and then you had wire mesh all around. I suffered terribly with claustrophobia and hated it when the last bit went on and we were caged.'

Fire-watching teams for duty in banks, churches, and public buildings were organised by the Civil Defence authorities. Not long after Eileen Wiggins married, she had to go and work at the Co-op in Widcombe Parade – her contribution to the war effort.

'I had a list of people at the Co-op who had to go fire-watching at the Co-op in Westgate Buildings. There was a fire-watching post in Green Park where there was a stirrup pump and an "incendiary bomb" for us to practise with. Upstairs at Westgate Buildings on the last floor, there was an iron ladder flush to the wall. One of the men was from the furniture department, and the other from the kitchen department. We had to do our duty all night. We used to arrive about 8 o'clock and stayed until about six next morning. We had to sleep in our clothes – I wore slacks – it didn't feel natural. We had a brilliant time. About 10 o'clock the men used to say, "Well, good night girls," and then go into their room. If there was an alarm, the men used to go up on the roof. I only ever went up once. And I did fire-watching right through the war.'

Eric Lanning, then a young member of the Abbey congregation and the Abbey Youth Fellowship, volunteered to fire-watch at the Abbey:

'It was pretty primitive in the early days. Stirrup pumps and buckets of water and a few sandbags were all that protected the Abbey from incendiary bombs. Later, a water main was run up to the roof level to provide an unlimited supply. We were a mixed bunch of "young men and maidens" who enjoyed doing this form of war work. We were strictly segregated in our sleeping arrangements. The girls had the luxury of sleeping in the clergy vestry, while the boys slept in a large tent erected in the ringing chamber in the tower.'

David Falconer's father (then in his late fifties) did regular fire-watching duties during the night at Lloyd's Bank at the top of Milsom Street.

Although his mother (then in her forties) undertook training, she never actually performed any duties. In an attempt to bestow some form of official status, armbands were issued by the authorities to all firewatchers.

In about December 1939, Pamela Taylor's father, Percy, was asked to become an air raid warden, 'looking out for fires' in the vicinity of Milton Avenue where they lived. He became a warden in the following year. 'Up came the ARP people with some tin hats for him. He had one himself and put the rest down in the basement of our house.'

In case of enemy air attack, first aid posts were set up across Bath to deal with the civilian casualties that were feared would follow a raid. One of these was at East Twerton. It was located in spacious premises adjacent to St Peter's church in Dorset Street, a few minutes' walk from the home and surgery of Dr Burke Cuppage, who was in charge. 'The post was manned by three squads who were on call, 1-in-3 during the day, and slept there at night.' Dr Cuppage was always on call at home during the night. 'Tim' Cuppage's mother led one squad, and her aunt, a refugee from Jersey staying with the family, led another. 'My mother decided that bending over stretchers in a skirt was undignified, and so she had some dark grey trousers made by my father's tailor. She looked very good in them! She was possibly the first woman of her type and generation not in uniform of any kind to sport trousers in Bath.'

St Peter's (East Twerton) First Aid Team pose for the camera early in the war. Dr Burke Cuppage (father of 'Tim' McConnell) is at centre front. 'Daddy' Croome is in the back row, second from the left. (*Tim McConnell*)

Dr Cuppage held regular training sessions at his post and, during her school holidays, 'Tim' 'spent many hours re-rolling bandages and packing them into metal drums to be sterilised':

> 'A strong sense of camaraderie developed among and between the squads, in which there were some great characters. Mr Croome [known as 'Daddy' Croome] always brought with him his gentle and delightful dog, of which my Father became very fond. And Mr Jack Tolman, who I think was the manager of the Blackett Press and lived in Junction Road, provided much wit, humour, and entertainment. I remember wonderful Christmas parties where a type of hockey was played among competing squads in the upstairs room.'

There was, of course, the serious side when the post became operational during the odd 'hit-and-run' raids and, later on, during the Blitz. 'Tim' remembers that during the Blitz her father 'had special praise for the post's messenger boys, who braved the streets on their bikes collecting information from ARP wardens and giving news of casualties to families. The name Roger Banks particularly springs to mind in this context.'

Searchlights were a familiar feature at night. Betty Cottle, living at Whiteway Circle in the end house, 'where they'd finished building', remembers a big field nearby:

> 'Up there was this trench with sandbags around it, and this is where they had this searchlight at Whiteway and Haycombe Drive. They used to come down to my Mum twice a day with a bucket for Mum to make them tea – they used to bring their own sugar and tea because everything was rationed. And they'd give my Mum a few coppers at the end of the week to pay for the gas. They used to put this searchlight on at night.'

There was also a searchlight battery at Lansdown, on the racecourse. Margo Cogswell remembers that: 'The only place I could see searchlights was when I lay in bed at my Grandma's house at Box, and these must have been at Colerne airfield. They were criss-crossing the sky as I peeped out of the blackout.'

Huge silver barrage balloons were another feature of the wartime sky, though not initially over Bath. Margo could always see them 'over Bristol, going right across the sky' from her home in Hensley Road.

David Falconer remembers lying in bed at night unable to sleep. 'I often heard the unmistakable sound of German bombers flying high over Bath, or very close to the city. Mother used to remark, "It sounds as though Coventry is in for it again tonight". Later, we sometimes heard the bombers returning from the raid, not in squadron formation as they went, but in ones and twos.'

Following the Secretary of State for War, Anthony Eden's call to arms on 14 May 1940, within two days more than 600 Bath men had enrolled for the Local Defence Volunteers (LDV). The Bath garrison was formed on 22 May and by August it had been renamed (nationally) as the Home Guard. At this point it was raised to battalion strength and comprised two battalions: the 5th Somerset (Bath City) and the 6th Somerset (Bath Admiralty) Battalions.

Members of the Bath Local Defence Volunteers (LDV) parade on Lambridge Recreation Ground in early July 1940. At far left is Bill Venn of Frankley Buildings, Camden, a letterpress machine minder for the *Bath Chronicle*, while at far right is Ernest Budge of Evelyn Terrace, Fairfield Park, who was a chef. The LDV was officially renamed the Home Guard on 22 July. The men are holding 'Long Lee' rifles – Rifle, Magazine Lee Enfield, forerunner of the more common SMLE. (*John Venn*)

Working for the Admiralty at Kingwood School, it was natural that Margo Cogswell's father should join the 6th Somerset (Bath Admiralty) Battalion in 1940. Across the road from their house in Hensley Road lived Mr Green, the manager of Bayer's, the corset manufactory on the Lower Bristol Road. Whenever the siren went, 'Daddy and Mr Green used to go off to see over the Bayer's factory to make sure everything was alright'.

Basil Williams, a young electrical engineer, came to Bath in 1939 to work with the Admiralty Department of Electrical Engineering at the former Royal United Hospital building (later Bath Technical College) in Beau Street. On the ground floor was the office, and in the basement were the experimental workshops which, in those days, were prone to flooding. Here, he joined a team that designed minesweeping equipment for installation in Royal Navy ships to foil the German magnetic mines that had been sown by enemy submarines and aircraft in the eastern coastal estuaries. Like others in the department, he soon joined the 6th (Bath Admiralty) Battalion: 'In addition to training and weekend exercises, we had to mount guard outside the building at night. Each section took their turn every fortnight when two of us stood outside the building on two-hour shifts.'

Christina Brooks' father was in the Home Guard at Bath and she recalls one of the amusing training sessions in which he took part – one that has echoes of the famous television series *Dad's Army*: 'One of the exercises they carried out was to line up on top of the Dry Arch bridge, which used to cross the Warminster Road at Bathampton and practice "bombing" lorries passing underneath, with bags of flour....'

In 1941, 15-year-old Bob White lied about his age to join the 5th (Bath City) Battalion – but for a very good reason, as he explains:

> 'I was with the Headquarters Company. We had our HQ in Monmouth Place, which is now Davies the painter and decorator's premises. We had all that building and we had a little rifle range in there. I joined because I had become a member of Hampset Cricket Club and I played in one of the original games. When it was formed, three or four people were involved and they were all from the City of Bath Boys' School, but I was a bit young – they were all 16 or 17-year-olds.
>
> 'They decided they wanted somebody to become the president of the club, so apparently they looked in the telephone directory and found this lieutenant-colonel. He had a double-barrelled name and was a bank manager, so they went to see him and asked if he would be president of our cricket club. After a bit of thought he said, "Yes, if most of you will join my Home Guard". About eight or nine of us joined and we became the Cycle Section of the Headquarters Company, which meant we went everywhere on our cycles.
>
> 'I remember that it was quite a cold winter [1941–42] and can recall being up on Lansdown and trying to ride my bicycle across the top there in six inches of snow carrying messages all over. We were young and it was great fun. We used to do a lot of exercise and got to know Wellow, Midford and Hinton Charterhouse very well.'

The Home Guard and the ARP had a combined post on top of Twerton Roundhill. Eileen Rogers remembers that, 'originally, they had a little wooden shelter, but it was replaced with a proper post with sandbags and all that. They must have had a good view of the Blitz from there.'

During her wartime school holidays, 'Tim' Cuppage and her friends (who were then aged upwards of 12 and 13) were expected to make a contribution to the war effort – they were considered old enough!

> 'A friend of my mother's, Mrs J.L. Palmer, wife of the manager of Bristol Tramways, recruited me and one or two of my friends as waitresses at the Toc H canteen for NCOs in Grove Street. I remember this as a hardworking, but very happy, experience: the men were so friendly, appreciative, amusing, and courteous. Mrs Palmer was an excellent and inventive cook who, among other things, produced jam tarts. I can

see them now! They were huge, glistening with brightly coloured jam, and decorated with pastry lattice. One of the bonuses was having lunch at the canteen while on duty.'

Mrs Palmer recruited 'Tim' and some other girls to make camouflage netting in a high-ceilinged room at the premises of Bristol Tramways, next door to John R. Huntley & Son, the provision merchants in Northgate (now occupied by the Podium). The nets were suspended from the ceiling, and they had to tie 'innumerable bits of brown, green, beige, and black rag to the mesh'.

Sometimes during the wartime summer holidays, to give her parents a break, 'Tim' and her family used to spend a week at the Jolly Sailor Inn at Saltford, which was near enough for Dr Cuppage to return to the practice and First Aid post in an emergency: 'The Inn, owned by a friend, provided a haven for war-weary folk and served very good food, thanks, I am sure, to dealings on the black market! Our rations at home were certainly supplemented by grateful patients from the country bearing produce – rabbits, game, vegetables, and eggs.'

Quite early in the war, David Falconer remembers that soldiers (other ranks) were billeted at Christ Church Hall, Julian Road. The officers were billeted in greater comfort at the nearby Bromley Hotel in Russell Street (now the Bloomsbury Hotel). 'I remember visiting the soldiers at the Church Hall and talking to them. They had no idea why they were in Bath, and did

Throughout the war, women played important and vital roles in the armed forces and the voluntary services on the Home Front. Here members of the Bath Branch of the Women's Voluntary Service (founded by Lady Reading) pose for the camera outside their headquarters in Quiet Street. Mrs Lilian Bankart, mother of one of the contributors to this book, Pat Woods, is at the extreme left of the picture. *(Pat Woods)*

not know where they were going next. Russell Street is quite steep, and it was amusing to see the soldiers lining up on parade there every morning. How they managed to steady themselves on the slope through their drill routines, I don't know.'

Dr Ted Matthews, writing two days after the declaration of war, summed up the general atmosphere.

> 'This is a most peculiar war and as different from the 1914 affair as one could possible imagine. There is no exuberant patriotism, no flag wagging or cheering crowds, yet every man woman & child is calm and determined.
>
> 'I have not heard a single person of the many hundreds of all political shades and opinions that I have spoken to who is not quietly and firmly determined to see this thing through whatever it may cost & whatever sacrifices it may mean. The morale of the people is beyond all things amazing. Great Britain is ready for anything and everything. The organisation of the various (& many) services is extraordinary.
>
> 'Even in a town like Bath, every few hundred yards has its fully equipped ARP warden's post with someone permanently on duty. Every anti-aircraft gun & searchlight has been mysteriously and silently put ready. Everyone has his gas-mask, every household has full instructions for every conceivable emergency, every window is blacked out – a most extraordinary effect at night when the whole country seems to be utterly dead and silent and, looking on the town from one of the hills, completely and absolutely black. All the kerbs and lamp posts have been painted white, and every road has a white line down the middle. Every car travelling at night is blacked out except for a mere glimmer of sidelights.
>
> 'Troops collect and vanish, there is no rush to buy food nor any shortage of anything. Up and down the town people quietly dig trenches in their gardens, or make gas-proof rooms as if it were the most ordinary thing in the world. Everyone in the street carries their little cardboard box with its gas-mask. Every policeman has his tin hat and gas mask slung on his back.'

CHAPTER 3
THE WAR GETS UNDERWAY

Early on in the war, the young Eric Lanning and his father, who was a keen photographer, were involved in an exciting incident. They were walking along the bank of the Avon some way below Pulteney weir and, as the light was perfect, Eric's father decided to take a photograph of the picturesque view of the weir and Pulteney bridge.

'Suddenly, we were approached by military (Naval) policemen and invited to accompany them to the Admiralty offices at the Empire Hotel where we were interrogated. After questioning and establishing that we were not spies, we were released, but not before the roll of film had been confiscated. What we had not appreciated was that we might have photographed fortifications in the shape of barbed wire barricades adjacent to the weir and below the hotel. A good example of security consciousness.'

With the fall of France in June 1940, the Phoney War was suddenly over and 330,000 troops, mainly of the British Expeditionary Force and French Army, were evacuated to England from Dunkirk. The miraculous rescue operation, undertaken by shoals of 'little ships' and naval vessels, was vividly described by John Masefield in his book *The Nine Days Wonder*, published in the following year. There appear to be few people in Bath now with clear memories of this great event, but former Bath schoolteacher Muriel Elmes considered it 'the greatest piece of English history':

> 'How I loathe the Frenchman Antoine de Saint Exupéry. He said that the English had deserted the French and were just making for England. He maintained that we had left the French to their fate. If he spoke the truth, he knew very well that the "little ships" took as many French as English back to England.'

As spring turned into summer the Battle of Britain unfolded in the skies over southeast England, fought between the Royal Air Force and the Luftwaffe. The relentless aerial onslaught was intended by the Germans to seize control of the air from the RAF before launching Operation 'Sealion' – the invasion of Britain. With the threat of imminent invasion, tensions across the country were running high. In common with many other people, Joan Barlow, together with a friend, became an 'Invasion Spotter'.

Among the British 'secret armies' during the war were the local Auxiliary Units of the Home Guard. Frank Mawer served in the 6th Somerset (Bath Admiralty) Battalion, as well as the secret Auxiliary Unit. The latter is pictured here to mark its stand-down in 1944. Seated centre (wearing glasses) is Captain Leonard Aves, Group Commander. (*David Carroll*)

'I think this was organised by the WVS. We had to leave the hostel at Weston Park in the morning in the dark and walk to the Holburne Museum at the end of Pulteney Street where we arrived before dawn. We went to a balcony on the outside of the first floor where we had to sit and watch a point in the far distance [the Home Guard-ARP post at Twerton Roundhill]. If there had been an invasion, cones would have been hoisted and we were to hoist similar cones to the ones we could see. They were balls, cubes, squares, etc. I think we were on duty for about an hour, then we went to our offices. I cannot remember how often or for how long we carried out these duties.'

Quite early in the war, Frank Mawer joined the 6th Somerset (Bath Admiralty) Battalion. A short time later he found himself involved in something infinitely more exciting than ordinary Home Guard duty. One day when he was working at Foxhill he was asked by his boss to go and see a Commander Morrison at the Francis Hotel in Queen Square. He felt that something special was afoot. On his arrival at the Francis, Frank met Commander Morrison, who closed his door, sat down at his desk, and said:

'"I am now going to talk to you about something which, if you don't want to join up with it, I just trust you will forget all about, and I'm not going to hold it against you." So this went on and, by jingo, to a young chap it was far better than just routine Home Guard stuff. I said I would join up, and I was told to report to Mr W.T. Aves – he was a contracts officer, I think [Captain Leonard Aves, Group Commander]. We were then told that we were to be issued with pistols, and we weren't to be like the ordinary Home Guard. My own unit would have a secret base. "You'll be out in the fields in the Kelston area", we were informed. In point of fact it was Kelston Hall. One day, when the Army took us there, we were told, "You are now within 25 yards of the entrance to your hideout. Find it!" And being unable to find it, we were asked, "Aren't you glad you couldn't find it?" Then we were taken down to this place where we saw that they'd staked out for us a floor, some bunks, and all the Mills bombs and plastic explosives that, at the time, the Army hadn't even got themselves, including "time pencils" [fuses]. Later we were taught how to use this ammunition.'

Frank had become involved in a special Auxiliary Unit of the Home Guard – a section of Churchill's so-called 'Secret Army', the purpose of which was to carry out sabotage work behind the lines in the event of a German invasion. Throughout the country that summer, other battalions of the Home Guard also had auxiliary groups with designated areas to watch, and all members were sworn to secrecy.

The Auxiliary Units were allocated to three new Home Guard battalions in England, Scotland and Wales during late 1942 – 201, 202 and 203 GHQ Reserve. No 203 GHQ Reserve Battalion included all Groups south of the Thames, from Kent in the east around to the River Severn in the west. The Bath area had two Auxiliary Units, one of 12 such groups in Somerset.

Somerset Group 1 – Admiralty, with five patrols: Kelston Park, Langridge, Warminster Road, Prior Park and Newton Park, with up to 20 men in each patrol.
Somerset Group 2 – City of Bath, with six patrols: Bathampton, Englishcombe, Midsomer Norton, Southstoke, Swainswick and Weston, with anything from 4 to 10 men in each.

Initially, Frank's group (Group 1, Kelston Park Patrol) had an establishment of six men, including a second lieutenant and a sergeant.

This post-war certificate commemorates the unsung role played by the Somerset Group of Auxiliary Units. (Frank Mawer)

THE WAR GETS UNDERWAY

Members of the Southstoke Platoon of the 5th (Bath City) Battalion, Home Guard, receive instruction in the handling of a Sten gun. (*Private collection*)

After extensive training exercises, opposing sides soon learnt each other's methods and, because of this, Frank remembers that 'things became absolutely frustrating'. It was then decided that they would do 'something different'. At that time there were two woods above Sham Castle, and Frank's group were told that they would have opposing them a company of the Admiralty Home Guard battalion that would be armed but without ammunition. Frank's group, on the other hand, would be unarmed, with the exception of a Ross rifle to be used for signalling purposes. 'We were told: "Your task is to get rid of those people from that wood, and we'll see how long it takes you". And we cleared that wood in ten minutes, which showed us that it could be done. I remember our officer just managed to catch a butt from one of the tommy-guns. But they were so frightened!'

During that eventful summer, Patricia Bankart, her brother, and a friend, decided to take a picnic in the fields on Box Hill:

'We had settled ourselves in the middle of the field, complete with tablecloth, tea and sandwiches. Suddenly, my brother announced that the two low-flying planes coming towards us were German fighters! I thought it ridiculous and that he must be mistaken. But, sure cough, when they flew over us we could see the German markings. We scattered immediately and ran for cover against a wall at the top of the field. The German pilots decided to return and have a closer look at us. After circling once more, they continued their journey. No harm was done, but it was quite a scary experience.'

At mid-summer 1940, Eric Lanning wrote an account of his first air-raid:

'My first air raid took place at 12.15am on Tuesday June 25th 1940. The air raid warning went at 12.15am just as the National Anthem was ending at the end of the 12 o'clock news bulletin. Daddy was listening to the news hoping to hear the Italian terms of peace. Gordon and I were in bed, both of us just dozing, when Gordon said he thought he heard the siren. Daddy switched off the wireless, and sure enough Gordon was right. The rumbling notes of the siren continued for two minutes. In the meantime, Daddy, to my mind very foolishly, stood in a doorway leading to the passage, Gordon crawled under my bed, and I pulled a small bookcase away from the wall and, taking two pillows and an eiderdown, I lay down behind the bookcase.

Eric Lanning, aged 20, at Bombay in 1942, the year of the Bath Blitz. Eric was then a subaltern in the 6th Gurkha Rifles of the Indian Army. (*Eric Lanning*)

'Ten minutes later the peculiar sound of the German aircraft engines was heard. It flew over Bath and we heard a burst of machine-gun fire from the plane, and then the noise gradually died away. We all thought that it was looking for Bristol. After circling over Bath and the neighbourhood for about two hours, in which time we had all gone to back to bed, we suddenly heard twelve distant "clumps". The sound seemed to come from the Keynsham and Bristol district about 10 miles away. Shortly after the "crumps" the German plane came back towards Bath. The noise now was much louder than it had been all through the raid. It was obvious that the Nazi, his job done, was beating it for home. That was the last we heard of him. At about 2.45am the "all-clear" was sounded, and so to bed.

'It was a beautiful night and absolutely first-class for a raid. The moon was shining and the stars seemed brighter than usual. Epilogue: according to the news bulletin today, five people were killed in a "south-western town" and there were 14 other casualties. According to local reports the bombs dropped on some of the suburbs of Bristol, Brislington and Temple Meads.'

Bath and its citizens were rarely troubled by the desperate air battle raging over southern England that summer. On a few occasions when

THE WAR GETS UNDERWAY

German aircraft were spotted flying over the city on their way to bomb Bristol or South Wales (or which had simply lost their way), their presence made an impression on Bathonians. The distinctive rhythmic throb of their de-synchronised engines is a sound that lodges in the memories of many.

Miss Sidney Lloyd, who lived in Park Lane, was a firewatcher whose 'patch' included the Gas Works and part of Weston Road. She noted in her diary the frantic air activity over the city on Wednesday 25 September, a day that had dawned with a typical autumnal haze clearing to produce fine but cloudy weather with sunny intervals – ideal, in fact, for a daylight bombing attack, the cloud banks offering German raiders welcome cover from British defences.

> 'Day Raid. 10.00 – 10.15am. Planes over 11.40 – 12.5am. Heavy gunfire to N. Large number of planes over Lansdown & dogfight overhead. I counted ten together and saw AA shells bursting & machine gun fire above Weston.'

David Falconer, then aged six and at school in the Paragon, remembers going home for lunch one day that summer and his mother telling him that she had seen many aircraft flying in the area of Beechen Cliff from the direction of Bristol. These were quite probably German aircraft returning to their bases in France from the Bristol raid, hotly pursued by RAF fighters.

Pages from the personal diary of Bath fire-watcher Miss Sydney Lloyd, who lived in Park Lane. The entries record enemy air activity over the city on Wednesday and Thursday 25 and 26 September 1940. (*Bath Reference Library*)

Although of poor quality, this rare photograph shows Sqn Ldr Peter Devitt's 152 Squadron Spitfire that he force-landed at Newton St Loe on 25 September 1940 after a running fight with a German Heinkel He 111 bomber that had just bombed Filton.

A combat report filed by Spitfire pilots of the RAF's 152 Squadron immediately upon landing back at their base at Warmwell in Dorset, recorded in brusque detail the deadly duels that had unfolded in the autumn skies over Bath that Wednesday lunchtime. A large formation of German Heinkel bombers had successfully penetrated the British defences and made a devastating but unopposed assault on the Bristol Aeroplane Works at Filton, north of Bristol, claiming 238 casualties from the factory's workforce. Pilots of 152 Squadron had eagerly intercepted the German bombers of Kampfgruppe 55 and their Messerschmitt Bf 110 fighter escort from Zerstorergeschwader 26 as they headed for home over Bath.

> '100-plus Ju 88, He 111, Me 110, Me 109. 11.30 – 12.00 S of Bristol. 15,000 ft. Blue 1 [Squadron Leader Devitt, officer commanding 152 Squadron] leading 4 aircraft of B Flight intercepted 100-plus enemy aircraft over Bath. Enemy aircraft flying south. Blue 1 ordered No. 1 attack closing to quarter on a vic of 3 Ju 88s on right flank. Blue 1 saw incendiaries hitting centre of Ju 88s closed to 20 yds and although he damaged enemy aircraft was unable to observe results as he was blinded by petrol from punctured tank, which caused him to force-land.'

The German bombers were in fact Heinkel He 111s and not Junkers Ju 88s as mistakenly believed by the RAF pilots. Escaping petrol from Devitt's fuel tank, punctured by return fire from the He 111, temporarily blinded him. Uninjured, he managed to force-land his Spitfire at Newton St Loe on the western outskirts of the city.

Like most young boys of the time, Bob White from Milton Avenue was fascinated by aeroplanes. His school, the City of Bath Boys', situated near the top of Beechen Cliff, afforded excellent views across Bath and he remembers watching the German bombers flying across the city on their way to attack Filton:

'We were at school and when the siren sounded we were supposed to disappear to our homes or to another house nearby. On that particular day we just stood there and watched them – mostly Heinkel 111s and a few Spitfires shooting at them. We stood and watched them disappear towards Bristol. We saw them coming back, not in any particular formation, they were all split up. There was one Spitfire that crash-landed at Newton St Loe. Of course, we all went down to have a look at it but you couldn't get anywhere near it. There were too many guards.'

High above, the action drifted south towards Frome, leaving Bath beneath a fast-fading swirl of white chalk marks in the sky. Within a few minutes, one of the pursuing Spitfires, flown by Sergeant Pilot Kenneth Holland, was seen by Pilot Officer Bayles to crash near Frome. Following a running dogfight in which Spitfires and Hurricanes seriously damaged a Heinkel He 111 flown by the Staffelkapitän of KG55, Sergeant Pilot Holland was delivering the coup de grâce when he was shot through the head by a single bullet from the Heinkel's rear gunner. Both aircraft crashed at Woolverton on the Wiltshire–Somerset border shortly after midday. Sergeant Pilot Holland was killed.

Sergeant Pilot Kenneth Holland, also of 152 Squadron, attacked German bombers over Bath on 25 September, but later he was shot down and killed at Wolverton, near Frome. Holland was an orphan from Australia who had been adopted by a couple from Camelford in Cornwall.

During the night that followed, targets in London, north-west England and North Wales were bombed. At Bath, Miss Sidney Lloyd recorded in her diary: '9 – 12.15am. Planes over at 11.45 & searchlights to N. 4.10 – 5.10am. planes.' And when the day was over aircraft losses stood at RAF (4) and Luftwaffe (13).

By the end of October 1940, the Battle of Britain had been all but won by the RAF, but the spectre of Luftwaffe night blitzes over Britain soon became a frightening reality, as Bathonians were later to discover.

Writing from his home at Newbridge Hill to his daughter Bridget in New Mexico on 5 December 1940, Dr Ted Matthews may have been tempting Providence when he recounted to her that 'we had a bad raid here a few nights ago, but although there was a lot of noise and several bombs were dropped all over the place, no-one was hurt. I think there is a special angel who looks after Bath. We seem to get all the excitement without getting any casualties.'

WARTIME BATH: LIFE ON THE HOME FRONT 1939-45

Sometimes, men of the Bath Auxiliary Fire Service at Cleveland Bridge were called out in times of manpower shortage to help their colleagues during the heavy air raids on Bristol. Ray Burgess took a Bath crew to Bristol on 2 December 1940, where he found the city in chaos:

> 'I went to the central fire station [in Nelson Street] and all the doors were out – down flat. There was one man in the place and we told him we were reporting with five men and a lorry loaded with hose. "Where do you want it?" I asked him. "Just go round the corner, there's a big fire burning round there. It might be useful there." But that's what happens when the communications go down.'

Although there were frequent 'alerts' during the early part of the war, very little action was seen in Bath. Joan Hurford remembers an occasion when:

> 'Mum took my sister Betty and me to the Scala Cinema in Oldfield Park to see Judy Garland in *The Wizard of Oz*. While we were

The staff of the Royal London Mutual Assurance Society parade for the camera outside their offices at the intersection of Charles Street and Kingsmead Street early in the war. By this time, Lita Elliott's father, who was Assistant Superintendent of the Society, had joined the forces. The staff seen here are in the uniforms of the various Civil Defence organisations in which they had volunteered to serve. Unfortunately, it has proved impossible to identify any of these people. (*Hester V.M. Elliott*)

returning home to Widcombe via the Lower Bristol Road, the siren went. We were hustled into an air raid shelter with other people until the "all-clear" sounded. I remember we were rather apprehensive about sitting there with strangers, wondering what would happen. But, gradually, as the war progressed, we had many apparent false alarms, and people didn't bother to take shelter anymore.'

At some time in 1940, Eric Lanning remembers what may have been the first bomb to be dropped within the city boundaries. It fell on allotments on the High Common, about 100 yards from his home in Cavendish Crescent:

'The only damage caused was by blast. A number of the upper windows in the Crescent were shattered, the lower ones were protected by the garden wall of Cavendish Lodge. Until fairly recently, the shrapnel damage could be seen on the wall. This being the first bomb, many of the good citizens of Bath walked up the hill to survey the damage.'

Also in 1940, Eric was walking along the Royal Crescent on a winter's day when the cloud cover was thick and 'hovered a few hundred feet above the city': 'Suddenly, there was a loud noise, and bursting through the cloud was a German bomber – probably a Heinkel – which proceeded to drop a bomb, which I could see quite clearly. I learnt later that the bomb had landed in Weston, but because of the low angle had not exploded, and bounced along the ground.'

Perhaps this was the incident witnessed by the Newbridge GP, Dr Ted Matthews, and described by him in a letter to one of his daughters on 5 December 1940:

'The other afternoon I was sitting in the Surgery and I heard an aeroplane flying quite low. It was a beastly afternoon, drizzling with rain and with a fine mist hanging over the town. I went to the Surgery door and looked out and saw a large plane flying low down towards me, and as I watched I saw two things drop out of it. For a moment I didn't realise that the two things were bombs, but a moment later I heard them whistling through the air. Half the children were out in the garden and I rushed down to see if I could get them in, expecting to hear a terrific explosion. The air seemed to be full of whistling bombs, but there were no explosions and by the time I had collected the children, the plane had vanished into the mist again. The plane dropped eleven bombs all round this district, and not one exploded. Some fell through the roofs of houses, but no-one was hurt.'

The first Bath civilian casualties of the war were sustained at Twerton where a stick of stray German bombs fell on 16 March 1941 killing three men and three evacuee children. The siblings Doris, Ellen and Robert Randall, the youngest of whom was six years old, died in their beds at 8 High Street when an HE bomb demolished two adjoining houses. Two others in the same house were injured. Flying shrapnel also killed two men who were walking in the street outside, while a third adult nearby was also injured and died on his way to hospital.

Less than a month later, eleven people lost their lives in the Dolemeads on the night of Good Friday/Easter Eve, 11 and 12 April 1941, when another stray stick of bombs fell on Excelsior Street, Princes Buildings and Broadway during the course of a major night attack on Bristol. The death toll included two infant girls and two married couples. For Bathonians, this was the worst raid of the war so far and the *Chronicle* was restricted in the choice of photographs that it could publish to illustrate the destruction. The censor considered that many of the scenes of devastation captured by the paper's photographer were likely to be damaging to public morale and forbade their publication.

Joan Potter and her family were living in the Widcombe area at the time: 'My grandmother, who lived with us, was stone deaf and bedridden. After the bombs dropped my mother went into her bedroom. She was surrounded by the window frame and glass that had blown out during the

 Danger: unexploded bomb. Early in the war a bomb, which failed to explode, was dropped in the meadows near Bathampton Manor. As a safety precaution, the area was cordoned off. In this photograph, A. White (Special Constable), Len Snell, and Donald Hamilton (Senior Warden) stand guard in the road near St Nicholas's church. (*Brian Hamilton*)

explosion. My grandmother said, "We must have had a very bad storm in the night!"' Sometime after the event, Emma Hinge, a 40-year-old resident of Broadway, told John Coe how she had been fast asleep when the bombs were dropped: 'When she was woken, she could not understand why she could see stars above her head. It took her some moments to realise that the whole roof had been blown off, and debris was piled everywhere.'

Mary James, living with her mother and father at King Edward Road, came home from school one afternoon some time before the Blitz and saw a plane circling overhead and dropping bombs. 'They were dropped from such a low level that they didn't explode. It appears that the bombs dropped on the Gas Works. One night along Englishcombe Lane they had a series of incendiaries, but fortunately it was mostly fields there.'

And one day an incendiary bomb fell in Faulkland Road where Ray Burgess lived: 'It hit the coping and landed in the front garden, and the next-door neighbour came round. I wasn't there, nor was Audrey's father.

The Bathampton ARP and Civil Defence squads had their headquarters at The Trossachs in Warminster Road. This photograph dated 26 October was taken early in the war by Cyril Howe, the well-known Bath photographer. Front row: Bowell, -?- , Donald Hamilton, Joseph Plowman (later a Bath Alderman), Colonel Robert Hutchings, Albert(?) Blanchard, John Noad. Middle row: ? Wheeler, ? Date, -?- , ? Masterman, -?- , -?- , ? Knight, ? Boroughs,. Back row: Norman Hunt, Len Snell, -?- , ? Harwood, -?- , Albert Hawkins, Reginald Netherwood. (*Brian Hamilton*)

Our neighbour dug the earth up and put it out. Then, what was left of it was stolen in the night!'

There was great excitement in 1941 when a high explosive bomb fell in a field near Bathampton Manor. Brian Hamilton recalls that it failed to explode:

> 'I will always remember it because my father was the senior warden at the Civil Defence and ARP post at The Trossachs, Colonel Hutchings' residence, in Warminster Road. He and another warden, Jack Noad, set out to see exactly where the bomb was. Soon after they left, the phone rang and somebody at ARP HQ asked if they would go and read the marking on the bomb. So I, aged 10, got on my bike and rode down towards the Manor to deliver the request. I don't know which of them was the more horrified to see me! Before I'd even got the message to them, they both greeted me with a torrent of abuse, telling me to go back home. Eventually, when I told them why I'd come, they were even more annoyed! They quickly set up road-blocks, and gave me a very explicit message to phone back to HQ stating that whoever asked for such information should ****** come and do it themselves! Later that day, a bomb disposal team arrived and successfully defused the bomb.'

A further year was to elapse before Bath would be shaken to its very foundations.

This rare pre-war photograph of Kingsmead Square in 1922 at its intersection with Kingsmead Street, looking towards Charles Street in the distance, reveals a vista that was swept away after the Baedeker Blitz. Kingsmead Street, where Lita Chivers lived with her brother and parents, suffered extensive bomb damage and much loss of life.

CHAPTER 4
BLITZ WEEKEND

After tea on 25 April 1942, people followed their usual Saturday evening routines – going to a dance at the Pavilion, watching a picture at the Forum, or perhaps visiting friends and relations. Or, simply staying at home. It was like any other wartime Saturday night.

After playing tennis, Mary James returned to her terrace house at King Edward Road in Oldfield Park and went up to bed just before 11 o'clock. Sometime later, while she was undressing, the siren went.

On the other side of the river, 'Dudu' Morgan, a young Admiralty worker, and her friend Pam with whom she shared a bedroom, were billeted in a house in Great Bedford Street, off Julian Road near St Andrew's church:

> 'The last one of us to go to bed used to open the window shutters. That night I was last in bed and I had opened the shutters to reveal a lovely moonlit night. We could hear all the planes in the distance, and I said to Pam, "Wouldn't it be funny if they settled on Bath!" And I'd hardly finished saying in when the first bomb came. I never slept in a nightie and so I got out of bed naked, grabbed my housecoat off the peg and struggled to put it on. And everyone in the house rushed down to the cellars. As we were going down, I fell, and I got my housecoat half on so I was half-naked – it was pitch black, fortunately! I'm sure I trod on somebody – I don't know who it was. By the time we'd got a light down in the cellar, I'd got it on, fortunately!'

For 22-year-old Freda Beatty billeted in Englishcombe Lane, her evening meant making her way down to the Abbey to do her fire-watching duty with another young woman and two young men from the Abbey Youth Fellowship. They met in the clergy vestry where they made hot chocolate with powdered milk. Later, the young men went to bed in the ringing chamber in the tower while the girls bedded down in the vestry, which was 'blacked out'.

Since the war had begun, Bath people had become accustomed to hearing enemy aircraft flying over the city to bomb Bristol. In fact between May 1940 and August 1941, a period of fifteen months, it was recorded that Bath endured a staggering 875 red alerts,

German twin-engined Dornier Do 217 bombers flew many sorties over Bath during the Blitz weekend.

but only a few bombs landed on the city, and even they were not meant for Bath. When the sirens wailed on that Saturday night at about 11pm, they thought that once again Bristol was 'going to get it'. Ray Burgess of the AFS remembers that 'lots of fire appliances had already left for Bristol when it [the bombing] started in Bath'.

From her home in Albany Road in Twerton, Phyllis Bond could see that it was a beautiful moonlit night. 'There were of course no lights visible anywhere, but the moon was so bright we didn't need any. Then we heard "Jerry" coming over. Nothing unusual in that because they were always flying over to Bristol and occasionally dropping their load [on Bath].'

Fourteen-year-old Pamela Taylor, a schoolgirl at the City of Bath Girls' School in Oldfield Park, had been playing tennis that afternoon on the school courts. Elsie, her stepmother, and her father Percy had come along to watch. She remembers Elsie saying, 'I don't know, but I reckon we shall have it tonight! Exeter has had it.' That night when the alert sounded they went down to their cellar to take shelter. 'You could just about stand up in it,' she recalls. 'We sat in deck chairs.'

In the bright moonlight, flares from the leading German pathfinder aircraft cascaded down upon the unsuspecting city shortly before 11.20pm, their task being to mark and illuminate the target for the following main force of bombers. Moments later the first sticks of high explosive and incendiary bombs hit the streets of Bath in a raid of pure terror that was to last some 50 minutes.

Dr Sammy Marle, a Lansdown GP, and his friends were quietly playing their usual Saturday night game of bridge at the home of Dr Burke Cuppage in Victoria Buildings on the Lower Bristol Road when suddenly they heard a plane go over. Marle exclaimed, 'That's a Hun!' Shortly afterwards came a bang, 'and that's a bomb!'.

> 'With that the sirens sounded, so we hastily said goodnight and crept into Levis' car to take us home (Admiral Hughes, John Levis [surgeon] and myself). A couple of bombs fell by the Midland Station as we went by. Queen Square was full of people in night array going into a shelter. Then two more bombs rather close went off behind my consulting room (somewhere in Circus Mews) as we turned to pass No 19 The Circus. And the High School seemed well alight as we passed it by. The roads were already crackling with glass as we went up the hill. And then, some 40 yards above Lansdown Place East, we ran out of petrol. John refilled from a tin in the back while a Hun plane flew over machine-gunning and cannon firing wildly round about. Nothing came near us – I had switched out our lights! And then crash went another bomb just in front of Lansdown Place East. The blast was a distinct shock, though the explosion was on the other side of the terrace, and so with that, off we sailed again. Dropped Hughes at his home and so up the hill, where I found the family ensconced in the "strong spot" of the house and feeling not too cheery about it all. By this time it was evident Bath was taking it in the neck and, being undefended, the Hun came down very low to machine-gun roofs and windows, and many heavy (three lighter) bombs fell around the Lower Weston district – above the Upper Bristol Road, Gas Works, Stothert's, etc. There was already a big fire blazing in the Bristol Road as we passed up to Queen Square from the LMS station [Green Park]. And somewhere about 2 [am] the Hun went home.'

David Falconer (then aged eight) had spent the afternoon with Pat Henderson, their billetee's daughter, playing clock golf in Victoria Park. After a late tea he had gone to bed early. He remembers his father waking him suddenly and saying, 'Get up quickly, an air-raid has begun. The gas works have been hit.' David and his parents, together with their billetee Henderson and his wife and daughter, took blankets and pillows downstairs to the hall where they settled down against the wall under the staircase with Miss Dunkerton, an elderly maiden lady who lived in the ground floor flat. And then the noise began.

Locally-based RAF airmen pose with Betty Price, Phyllis Miles and Mary Paton in Parade Gardens during the summer of 1941. Phyllis was living with her husband Arnold in a flat at Morford Street during the Blitz. (*Phyllis Miles*)

'The whine of aircraft engines; the whistle of bombs falling followed by explosions, the rattle of cannon fire, the bells of ambulances and fire engines, the shouting of ARP personnel, and the screams of people running in the street outside. We were all terrified. In her fear and anxiety, Mrs Henderson was smitten with diarrhoea and kept running to the WC. At regular intervals we all prayed together, "O God, take care of us, and our friends and relations".'

Phyllis Miles and her husband Arnold who had married in the previous year were living in a ground floor flat at 11 Morford Street, off Julian Road, where artisans' terraced houses climb up steeply towards Belvedere on Lansdown Road.

'We were asleep when the first raid started and we got up out of bed straight away when the bombs started falling, so we didn't have a chance to put anything on, and we just dived underneath the bed. We were there for quite a long time. When it was over, we got dressed, and before we had a chance to make a cup of tea they were back again. I suppose, really, we were more prepared for it [this time] because on an occasion like this you think to yourself, you've got to be ready.

'There were five flats and there was a lady in the basement who I've been friendly with all my life – she went "berserk". We got into a little cupboard on the ground floor that was under the stairs, so you can imagine how big it was. There was seven of us in there

and we just had to stay there until the second raid was over. I don't think we realised what danger we were in. It doesn't occur to you when you're young like that. All the time I thought we'd come out of it and be OK. But it was really frightening, all those bombs. On the morning after the raid the air smelled acrid, it was horrible, you could smell the burning that had been going on.'

Mary James and her parents had one billetee living with them at their home in King Edward Road:

'We had no shelter but under the stairs was an outside wall, which had been recommended to us to use as a shelter. We had a gap when the "all-clear" went in the middle of the night, but my father went down to Moorland Road to check on his shop in Shaftesbury Road. It was still there, except the window had gone. And then the siren went again, so he left to come home, which wasn't very far. Someone called out to him from the air-raid shelter opposite the Scala, "Would you come in? Come into the shelter." He said, "No, I'd rather get home to my family." That shelter had a direct hit and I knew some people in there who were killed.

'Of course, he came home and we were all downstairs lying on the floor, and down came a bomb. It struck the middle of the terrace, and the church further up, which was my church, had a direct hit.

 The Scala on Shaftesbury Road, Oldfield Park, was a cinema from 1920 to the early 1960s when it became a Coop supermarket. A direct hit on a public air-raid shelter opposite the Scala on the corner of Shaftesbury Road and Third Avenue at 4.00am on 26 April claimed the lives of 16 civilians and 4 special constables in the adjacent Police Post.

I don't think you hear the actual bombs that are very close to you, but you hear them in the distance. When my father said to get out after the bombing, we heard a plane coming down and using its guns on the population. Whether they couldn't aim I don't know, but I didn't hear of anyone who had been actually struck that way. We went over to the house on the opposite side that I knew had a very strong wooden table at the back, in the back room. I went under the table.

 A memorial garden has been created on the site of the tragedy that obliterated the public air-raid shelter and Police Post.

'They had a daughter and we were at school together. When morning came I felt I was suffering from shock for a couple of hours. I can remember seeing the damage that had happened in our street. The next I can remember I had gone to a friend's not far away where we had a rest and they provided us with breakfast. But, of course, we carried on as best we could. Our house wasn't demolished, but the ARP warned us we couldn't sleep in it. It was badly damaged: all the glass had gone, all the windows had gone, and if I'd been lying in bed I would have been killed because there was a stone from the new church on my bed! There was one little girl, I never knew her name, who lived somewhere in the middle of our terrace, who was brought out alive, but she was taken to a first aid post at Walcot and killed the next night.'

Brian Hamilton recalls that one of the first bombs fell on The Folly (the Grosvenor Brewery), a popular watering hole beyond Hampton Row, situated between the railway and the canal.

A Royal Engineers bomb disposal team pose for their photograph beside an unexploded German bomb in Lyncombe Vale. Presumably, the bomb (250 or 500kg) had been defused before the picture was taken! (C.A. Bastin)

'I cannot remember if the landlord [Alfred Burgess] was killed or suffered severe shock, but it was the lads from the ARP post at The Trossachs in Warminster Road who found him.'

John Coe, then an 11-year-old schoolboy living in a small boarding school on Widcombe Hill, was woken about 11pm by the siren. 'Peering from behind the blackout curtains, I saw the awesome sight of many flares descending. And very soon the high explosive bombs were falling. We children were hastily despatched to the dark cellar under the house. Two bombs in Prior Park Road blew out windows and damaged our roof.'

After getting home to his family, Dr Sammy Marle lay down, hoping to get some rest. But about 3am he had a telephone call from the Royal United Hospital asking him and John Levis to go there. He and Levis were to man an operating theatre together.

Dr Sammy Marle, the Bath doctor whose game of bridge was rudely interrupted by the first raid of the Blitz. On the Sunday morning, Marle and fellow doctor, John Levis, operated for nearly 12 hours without a break at the Royal United Hospital on casualties of the first two raids. ('Tim' McConnell)

'So down we went, had a look round the cases we had to do – marked off the casualties, how they should be dealt with, and then kicked our heels until John Bastow [orthopaedic surgeon] should finish in our theatre. Before he did so the jolly old Hun was overhead again – still in the same neighbourhood, dive-bombing, machine-gunning and cannon-firing, it seemed, everywhere. We were standing against the wall of the back corridor of the hospital in company with what seemed about 100 others. Soldiers, civilians, wounded (mild), and every time a whistle started – down they all flopped to the floor. 'Pon my soul, it was somewhat demoralising, and after half an hour I wanted to flop too – but didn't. It all seemed to be getting nearer and nearer – here and there a window shattered out and all the lights were put out as the blackout had gone. How or why we were not hit I cannot understand – neither RUH, Forbes Fraser, nor Cottage Hospital. All most mercifully spared. As the time for dawn approached, I kept going out to inspect, and kept the shelters informed how light it was (soon) getting. And then the theatre was free. So just as the Hun left for home, we started in and went on almost without a break for nearly 12 hours, when a Bristol team relieved us and we went home for a wash and some grub. Actually, we had a very successful day and did some good jobs of work, I believe.'

When the siren went on the Saturday night, Ray Burgess, an AFS fireman living in Faulkland Road, 'got on the old motorbike and hopped it to the station' at Cleveland Bridge. Before the war, Britain's fire service was made up of more than 1,000 separate brigades, each with its own command structures, methods and equipment. There was little or no coordination and inter-brigade cooperation was not easy. Although the National Fire Service was created in August 1941 to form a single unified force made up of all the various brigades, Bath's firefighters were to learn a hard lesson during the Baedeker Blitz. Said Ray Burgess:

> 'Mostly, it was the big fires that were left to burn out. An officer made the decision that it wasn't worth saving a church and St Andrew's actually burnt [on the Sunday night]. My outstanding memory of that was seeing in St James's Square a man come down the stairs with an ordinary bread container and water had been put in it, and he put this incendiary in there which was the last thing to do. It wasn't burning, but it could easily have started. Getting around the debris was difficult, but it was the shock I suppose, really. I couldn't believe it was happening. The fire station was full of people because outlying areas started coming in. When the bombing was over, the system was great because a powerful pump would be set in the Avon and the road was dug up and pipes brought underneath and, with relays, water could be piped to Lansdown. But, you see, prior to that in Bath we had flatbed lorries with a 500-gallon tank strapped to the top. That's OK so long as the road doesn't have holes, so with experience later these things were sorted. But, really, preparation was non-existent because cooperation was different between different authorities. When you come to the question of water supply, Combe Down, for instance, was a separate entity. The water mains there were no good at all. Once the first shock of the bombing was over, the cheerfulness and comradeship returned. But the unpreparedness from the fire service angle stands out in my mind.'

Sixteen-year-old 'Rocky' Rochester was a Civil Defence messenger based at the Wardens' Post on the top of Twerton Roundhill. He lived at the top end of Roundhill Park so it was not far for him to go on duty at the post. His task was to take messages to and fro between his and other wardens' posts on his bicycle during bombing raids.

> 'When the sirens sounded on the evening of the 26th/27th, I cycled to the wardens' post and reported for duty. Nothing happened in our area and when the all-clear sounded I returned home. The sirens sounded again, I got out of bed and went downstairs, got dressed, but in the dark I couldn't find my boots. This saved my life because I would have been cycling down the road when a bomb landed there, a second on a side road and a third across the other side of Roundhill Park, followed by machine-gunning. The windows had blown out and you could hear the bullets smashing the tiles.'

At the start of the raids most of the telephone links had been severed between the various wardens' posts across the city and Civil Defence

 These houses in Bloomfield Avenue were badly damaged during the second raid in the early hours of Sunday morning, 26 April. Nos 12 and 13 (left) were wrecked and have since been rebuilt. Nos 14 and 15 suffered extensive damage to their roofs, but the houses themselves did not require rebuilding. (*Basil Williams*)

Control at Apsley House on Newbridge Hill. This effectively made the Civil Defence Control centre redundant and great reliance was therefore placed on the Civil Defence Messenger Service to maintain vital communication links across the city. 'Rocky' Rochester again:

> 'As the phones were out of order I made the trip from the post to CD Control throughout the bombing. My closest mishap occurred as I was cycling towards the Windsor Bridge, past the gasworks, which were on fire. The going became so bad because of the debris in the road that I had to proceed on foot and carry my bicycle. It got worse as I reached the bridge, but because of the light from the fires I noticed that I was just about to fall into a bomb crater to one side of the bridge, with water at the bottom. The bomb had landed right on the edge of the bank. I continued to and fro all night carrying messages. As daylight came, the alternative route I had used (down Lansdown View) had an unexploded bomb on the corner of Albany Road and Lansdown View just before the railway bridge.'

Eileen Rogers' father, James, was a constable in Bath City Police. He was deaf as a result of his military service with the Grenadier Guards on the Western Front in the First World War. However, he was 'kept on' as a policeman, but his duties were normally restricted to office work at the station. However, if he was at home when the siren went, he had to go on duty immediately. Eileen explained:

> 'On the first night of the Blitz, Dad was sent down to Kingsmead Square – to Bush's Corner – which was just about one of the worst places he could have been. He was standing right there when Kingsmead Street went up. Of course, he was deaf, but he could still hear the terrible noise of the explosions and feel the vibration. The machine-gunning was the worst, I think, more so than the bombing. The bombing was the noise, but the machine-gunning was terrifying. Bath was so unprepared for this.
>
> 'There were not enough public shelters. Near to us there was one in Oldfield Park, and one down Coronation Avenue, I think, although the latter might have been a Wardens' Post. There was nowhere for us to run. We had to find the safest place in the house to shelter, the furthest away from glass, between the sitting room and the dining room. Five of us crouched in an area the size of a fireplace. This was the first time in my life that I had stared death in the face, when you actually think, "this is it". I remember thinking, "I'm whole, I'm normal, I'm healthy, and any second I could be completely blown to bits!" – and it's the most horrible, awful feeling. You just had to

accept that you either lived or you didn't. At that precise moment I couldn't see how anybody could have lived through the Blitz, not with it all raining down on you. It was absolute luck that we survived.

'It was very sad because, just opposite and a few doors down, a young fellow and his new wife whom he had married just a week before had come off their honeymoon, and their house had a direct hit and he was killed. He was buried in the rubble. But they did say that it was choking on dust that killed a lot of Blitz victims, including him.

'When these bombs dropped, according to the wardens up on top of Twerton Roundhill, who could see what was happening, as far as they could gather these bombers used the Roundhill like a marker. And they turned over there and swooped all along Englishcombe Lane and bombed, it would seem, on the way up in one direction, and on the return they machine-gunned. All our houses had chimneybreasts in the centre of the roofs, and each one had machine-gun bullets lodged in them.'

Police Constable James Rogers with his wife Margaret outside their home at 184 Englishcombe Lane. (*Paul Rosevear*)

Alison Selford was a 22-year-old journalist on the *Daily Worker* newspaper and a member of the Communist Party of Great Britain. (The *Daily Worker* was a Communist Party broadsheet newspaper for the working man and trade unionist.) In 1941, she joined the Civil Defence in Bristol as an ambulance attendant. Her personal experience of Bath's Civil Defence response to the bombing was not a favourable one, although the breakdowns in command and communication she describes were not dissimilar to those witnessed by Bath fireman Ray Burgess when he was sent to Bristol in December 1940 to assist the city's fire service:

'We in the Bristol Civil Defence were sent along to help Bath. There was only 12 miles between those two towns, but what a difference in outlook. The Bath Civil Defence had always thought this couldn't happen to them. There were all sorts of legends, for example that Mussolini wouldn't have Bath bombed because he was so keen on the Roman remains, and that the Germans wouldn't have bombed Bath because it had air pockets above it, which prevented planes from diving, or something like that.

And so these things were then generally believed and it was a complete shock and surprise when Bath really got bombed.

'When the Bristol Civil Defence was called in, we all had to stop and wait for our proper orders in a proper military manner at a village called Newton St Loe outside Bath. ... The village had a good view of Bath and we could see the whole city in flames ahead of us. ...

'In the middle of Bath there were a lot of evacuated families from London and Bath was full of children, and this was terrible for the rescue men. They were used to carrying dead bodies, but they were in tears because of these children, the dead children they were carrying.

'I was waiting to be told what to do. My job wasn't picking up dead bodies, my job was looking for live people who needed first aid. I was an ambulance attendant, so the driver of the ambulance and myself were directed to go and wait for further orders at the Bath ARP Headquarters. While we were there the bombers came back. ... Nobody was giving us any orders, which puzzled us very much. We were supposed to be taking our orders from the Bath Civil Defence and as we waited ... the heavy bombers came back and we all with one accord dived under the nearest solid thing, which happened to be a billiard table, and some flying piece of masonry hit me in the bottom!

'When we had picked ourselves up and dusted ourselves off, we were very surprised – where was this Bath Civil Defence who were supposed to give us orders, and we never heard a cheep out of them? And came the dawn and the all-clear (and the dawn didn't come very soon... a little before 6 as I remember) and we all came out to look at what was going on, and as the all-clear notes died away, out of a basement which we hadn't even known was there came these Bath Civil Defence people who should have been giving us orders.

'It turned out their morale had totally collapsed. This was one of the things that were not publicly mentioned at the time. They had completely lost track of what they were supposed to be doing and they only thought about saving their own skins and consequently we, the Bristol lot, including myself, had been left to face the bombs while these people who should have been giving us orders took shelter.

'And as the dawn came, which I hadn't thought I'd be alive to see, we looked at these deplorable characters from the Bath Civil Defence. It turned out that some rescue work had been going on in the city because one of the Bristol people had decided they weren't going to get any orders from the Bath people and he started giving orders himself and had taken over. But it was one of those deplorable episodes when I'm afraid the British people were not so splendid as we afterwards made ourselves out to be.'

In the centre of Bath, the Kingsmead area suffered extensive material damage and heavy loss of life from high explosive and incendiary bombs on both nights of the Blitz. The Chivers family, whose home was in Kingsmead Street, had a lucky escape on the Saturday evening, as Lita Chivers recalls:

'I had a friend in the WAAFs and with every leave she would ask me to visit her and her family at Newbridge Road and stay the night. Knowing that I would not be at home (my brother was already in the Fleet Air Arm), my mother and father went to stay with their friends

 Piles of rubble, the stink of smouldering damp wood, the air thick with stone dust from collapsed buildings – the scene on Monmouth Street looking towards Charles Street after the first two raids.

The same view today with Rosewell Court flats on the left, which were built on the site of blitzed Kingsmead Street, and Holy Trinity church (formerly St Paul's) in the background.

at Camden Road. Early on the Saturday evening we thought it was Bristol "having it". Instead we realised it was Bath. My friend's mother and sisters got into a cupboard under the stairs. My friend and I lay out in the passage with pillows under our heads and waited for it.

'With every bomb that fell we thought it would be for us. The dresser, filled with china, fell down with such a crash. Pictures fell off the walls, ornaments dashed everywhere. It was dreadful. Come 5.30am and it seemed we had been spared, so not knowing my mother had gone out and stayed for the evening with her friends (they couldn't have got home with the bombing anyway), I raced home praying they would be OK. We all arrived at the same time to find a land mine had gone off in Kingsmead Street. Our pet spaniel called Roger had been left in the house during the first raid, but miraculously he came out alive. He went to stay with our friends up at Camden.

'Much against the warden's advice we got back into the rubble and found one room not too badly hit. So, we gathered what furniture we could, put it into this room with the intention of sorting it out later, and went away to Camden Road. We need not have bothered, because the next night it was fire-bombed so we lost everything.'

'Bush's grocery shop had been bombed but it was rebuilt temporarily in Kingsmead Square around the big tree, and it was used by everyone.'

Just off the Bear Flat, Margot Cogswell and her family lived at 43 Hensley Road. Her father worked for the Admiralty at Kingwood School and was also in the Home Guard. They had two billetees,

WARTIME BATH: LIFE ON THE HOME FRONT 1939-45

 Basil Williams was living at Fir Lodge, 91 Bloomfield Avenue, at the time of the Blitz. Compared to the damage sustained by neighbouring properties, Fir Lodge escaped relatively lightly, but the effects of bomb blast blew in many of the windows, as shown in this photograph. Note the tape on the insides of the windows to minimise injury from flying glass. (*Basil Williams*)

an Australian and a Londoner. Usually, the billetees were not bothered when the siren went and used to stay in bed. Like many others, they believed that nothing much would happen in Bath:

> 'Of course, on the first night of the Blitz it did. My father called us all and we had to go down the trap door into the shelter in our cellar. And he said to Marjory, the Australian billetee, "Are you coming down?" "No", she replied, "no, nothing much will happen, and I'll sleep through it." Well, of course, the first bomb rocketed down BANG! And with all the tremours she was down over the trap door, and I don't think her feet touched the ground! Down in the cellar we had a Morrison shelter. There was my mother's maiden aunt, my mother and

 Egerton Road in 2021, looking towards No 2 (on the far right) from No 14 on the left. From a road of 15 houses, all suffered serious damage of which one (No 4) was totally destroyed and five (Nos 2, 6, 8, 10 and 14) were so badly damaged they were later demolished. (There are no odd-numbered addresses apart from No 1.)

father, me, my sister of 10 months old, and these two ladies, one of which was quite large – and also the puddles in the shelter!

'On the afternoon prior to this horrific evening, my father had been making a lawn. He had rolled it, raked it, and seeded it. In the middle of the night, when I woke up with all that was going on, I wanted to go to the loo, and my mother told me I had to go in a little potty in the shelter. I told her I wanted to go in the proper toilet, so my aunt took me up and we went all through the broken glass. The windows were all in, and the smell was dreadful. The lawn and everything else was completely shattered.

'I don't know what time of night it must have been, but in the early hours of the morning there was a tap-tap at the door. It was a group of ARP men coming to see if we were all right. They said they hated to tell us, but that there was an unexploded bomb in our back garden! When we came out of the shelter there was just a red glow in the sky and a terrible smell in the air. I was absolutely terrified by this. It was such a horrible, heavy, sulphurous smell, of soil and of houses that had fallen down, of masonry and dust. The air was still full of dust raining down from all the debris. The whole place seemed to be alight. With that we were all taken out and up to a lady called Mrs Lejeune's house [at 29 Hensley Road].

A 'little lady' Margot Cogswell knew at 4 Egerton Road perished in the Blitz: 'the road was flattened and her house with it'. (Susannah Watts, aged 93, died when her home, 'Rexholme', was totally destroyed. Her widowed daughter, Susie Sperring (67), who cared for Susannah at home, survived.)

The Kingsmead area pictured sometime after the Blitz when the rubble had been cleared. In the left foreground, the roofless houses of Seymour Street; towards the centre is the burned-out shell of Holy Trinity church on James Street West, gutted by incendiaries; behind is the wasteland of what was once Kingsmead Street, with Cross Lane linking through to Monmouth Street – today, occupied by Kingsmead car park and Rosewell Court flats.

'I remember when we were called out of our house to tell us about the bomb, we'd gone to bed with a fairly tidy house and got up in the morning and it's absolutely shattered to bits. The roof was off and the windows were out. My father said nothing was being done about the unexploded bomb, so he and Mr Green were going over to stay in the shell of the house and see if they could dig this thing out. Although my mother and Mrs Green pleaded with them not to, they dug and dug and found no UXB, just this huge piece of road that had come over from Egerton Road. We had a huge crater in the garden. Just as well it didn't land on the house! Opposite No 40, and down a bit on the waste ground, there was a public air-raid shelter, the one that you went down into and had the grass over the top.'

At Oldfield Park, Audrey Burgess, her parents, her sister and their grandmother spent the first night of the Blitz in the specially strengthened cellar of their house in Faulkland Road. Her husband Ray had gone on duty in the city with the Auxiliary Fire Service. 'The floor seemed to come up and you could feel the vibration under your feet. You could hear the sound of planes and the gunfire.' In the morning they found their ceilings had come down and their windows were blown in.

In 1942, Valerie Ford was a young child living with her family in a terraced house at 15 Coronation Avenue, just above the Ascension Church and South Twerton School. She has vivid recollections of the Blitz weekend, particularly the first two raids on the Saturday night:

'My father was on fire-watching duty at the Co-operative Society building in Coronation Avenue. As soon as the air-raid siren went, my mother, two brothers and myself used to take refuge in the larder situated under the stairs in our house where mother had placed a mattress for us. My father actually saw the bomb drop into the allotments at the back of Coronation Avenue, devastating the houses in Lymore Terrace and the lower part of Coronation Avenue, which were then gutted by fire. Only the fronts of the houses were left standing. When my father, who was very shocked, eventually reached our house he was relieved when we emerged from the larder. We were able to see the sky as the rest of the house had been devastated. The crater left by that bomb was large enough to take a double and a single-deck bus.'

The culprit that had wrecked the Fords' home in Coronation Avenue was a massive 1,000kg 'Hermann' high explosive bomb that had fallen in the allotments behind. It was so nicknamed because its bulbous shape resembled the German

 Repairs underway on the GWR main line at Twerton on 5 May 1942 after a bomb strike during the Blitz had destroyed a section of track and collapsed part of the viaduct wall. (*Mark Coath Wilson*)

Luftwaffe's corpulent Reichsmarschall Hermann Goering.

Across at Albany Road in Twerton, Phyllis Bond had taken to the street shelter after the siren had gone. 'One stick of bombs was dropped near us. One unexploded bomb dropped in Albany Road itself. Another dropped at the bottom of our garden where the GWR line was. Another dropped the other side of the line near the Lower Bristol Road.' On one side of the road there was a row of houses, Railway Buildings, which was soon blazing away following a hit. 'Everybody was in the shelters except one eccentric woman who barricaded herself into her house with her little dog. Eddie Coles, who kept a greengrocer's shop opposite, realised that she was in there, got a ladder and risked his life to get her out. Unfortunately, her dog died in the blaze.'

Sixteen-year-old Sylvia Hancock was living at 8 Railway Buildings with her father and mother, Wilfred and Beatrice, her sister Shirley aged 8, and brother Trevor (3).

> 'On the first night of the raids my dad was on ARP duty. We used to go under the stairs when the sirens went. It was then that we realised the top of our house was on fire. We managed to get out but they [the bombers] were machine-gunning all along the road – the Lower Bristol Road. We got in under the arches [opposite Twerton Retail Park] where there was already a crowd of people sheltering. We were there all night. In the morning we went back to Railway Buildings but there was nothing left of our house. Everything was gone. We were left with only what we were dressed in, which was our night clothes.
>
> 'The same night my dad lost his whole family in the shelter at Roseberry Road – his father, Albert Hancock, stepmother Daisy, and two stepsisters – Rita and Kathleen. It was ever so strange: about 4 o'clock I said to my mum, brother and sister "Grampy Hancock's here". That was the very time they were all killed in Roseberry Road.'

There were many tales of heroic work during the Blitz. Outstanding among them is the story, untold since it first appeared in the *Chronicle* several weeks after the raids, of two young members of the 5th Somerset (Bath City) Battalion Home Guard. During the first two raids, Private Frederick James Park, aged 17, and his friend Private Alan Woods, aged 19, were out from the start helping wherever they could. They directed people to air-raid shelters, aided rescue work and fire-fighting, and tended the wounded under a hail of machine-gun fire. Fred alone saved the lives of six people. Even through the dust and fury of the raid, Fred noticed a light burning brightly in a butcher's shop, got inside and extinguished the light. As he came out, two old women came struggling along the street, half-collapsed with terror, not knowing which way to turn to escape the inferno of the bombing. By half-dragging, half-carrying them, Fred managed to get them to cover.

It was during the second raid that a high explosive bomb fell on the grandstand at the Recreation Ground. The blast was so great that it blew in the great east window and dozens of other windows in the Abbey, more than 300 yards away. Freda Beatty was on due at the time in the ringing chamber inside the tower and was covered with fragments of plaster dislodged from the walls by the blast. Freda Whittern, her sister and their parents were living in the city centre at Church Street, in the shadow of the Abbey:

'The siren wailed. Mum and Dad called us to hurry. We slipped into our clothes and ran down the stairs into the street. Our nearest shelter was in Parade Gardens in cellars underneath the road. We found ourselves with lots of other people, some dressed, some still in their night-clothes. We were standing or sitting, just waiting for the "all-clear". Then I noticed a lady a short distance away with a beautiful Dalmatian dog. The dog was shivering with fright and, as I like dogs, I went over to stroke it. A growl, a snap, and there I was with a very nasty hole in my finger! Father was furious, the lady upset, the dog still frightened, and me shaking. After what seemed an eternity the "all-clear" sounded and I was rushed home, my finger painful and bleeding. Father was still angry, and mother was looking for the torch because our lights had fused. Father cleaned up the wound and then poured iodine into it. The finger healed eventually, but the scar and the memory are still with me today.'

During the Saturday night, Joan Barlow was fire-watching with other Admiralty colleagues at their Royal School offices on Lansdown:

'Fortunately, we had no bombs or fires at the school, but we could hear the bombers diving, the bombs exploding, and machine-gunning by the Germans. At the end of the night I returned to my hostel in

The south arm of Bloomfield Avenue pictured days after the Blitz. Basil Williams lived further down the road. Behind the hedge are the tennis courts where Mrs Edith Dando (who lived at No 52) was killed in tragic circumstances shielding her two daughters during the second raid in the early hours of Sunday morning, the 26th. (*Basil Williams*)

Weston Park down a back lane, passing bombed houses all the way. Eventually I reached a field where the only sound was a bird singing. It was unbelievable, after all the noise and terror of the night before. After breakfast, as it was Sunday, several of us went into Bath to the WVS office to offer help. In the morning we went to the fire station where we peeled potatoes. In the afternoon we were in one of the streets making sandwiches on a street barrow for bombed-out people.'

Joan Potter's uncle and his family lived on a farm at Shepton Mallett. On hearing of the first night's Blitz, her aunt rang their local butcher in Bath and asked him to get word to Joan and her sister, to go and stay with them. 'Mum and Dad seemed keen on the idea, but we both refused to leave them.'

During the second raid in the early hours of Sunday morning, 48-year-old Edith Dando of 52 Bloomfield Avenue was frightened because her husband was out on duty. She left the house and took her two daughters across to what she imagined would be the safety of the tennis courts. Pamela Taylor remembers: 'When a bomb fell nearby, she lay on top of the two youngsters but she was killed by the blast. Her husband was down at the Scala on fire-watching duty. He wasn't killed, but many people in the air-raid shelter there lost their lives.'

Terence Gay was a small boy of eight living with his family along the Lower Bristol Road at 12 Roseberry Road in East Twerton:

> 'We got through the first wave just with broken windows. My mother, my aunt and I went to visit my other aunt at New Road Buildings. When the second wave came they dropped flares and incendiaries as they passed. One came through the roof and set the bedroom ablaze. My uncle put it out and then we went to the shelter in Innox Park. As we came out of the house and crossed the main road, we were machine-gunned by approaching bombers. I could see the gunner quite clearly in the moonlight, he was in the nose turret of a Heinkel. I watched the bullets strike the road all around us.'

During the lull after the first raid, early on the Sunday morning, Sarah Heal ventured out of her home near Victoria Park to see if she could find out how her husband and his family were faring at their home in Oldfield Park. 'Walking down Marlborough Lane we passed many unfortunate people who had been shot by low-flying planes, although that fact didn't register at the time.'

Among many Bath residents who were to lose homes in the Blitz were the Taylors who lived at 'Melville' on Milton Avenue. Here, Pamela sits for the photographer with her father and stepmother at their home. (*Pamela Voysey*)

Similar thoughts of family were in the mind of Phyllis Bond, who was worried about her sister living at Broadmoor Park in Lower Weston:

'Once the "all-clear" had sounded, my brother and I, my mother and our lodger, decided to walk over and see if they were alright. We just got as far as the Halfpenny Bridge (at the back of the Flight Works factory linking Twerton with Lower Weston) when my brother pushed me to the ground and covered me with his body. Just then, another stick of bombs came raining down. Fortunately, they all fell in the river. Anyway, up we got and eventually arrived at Broadmoor Park. They had seen it all and heard the noise, but that side of Bath was not touched.'

Up on Bear Flat, Pamela Taylor of Milton Avenue and several other families from the avenues all walked over to Beechen Cliff and looked down on the fires in the town. 'There was an acrid smell in the air and in was awful to see the fires. You could hear the screams from the flats in Green Park below. Dad said, "We are going to get it" and he wanted to get the car out and go into the country. But mum wouldn't have it, saying, "We shan't get any more now".

About a quarter to five on the Sunday morning when the sirens went again, Pamela Taylor didn't want to get up, but her father made her. 'I dressed, put on a shirt, but wouldn't put any shoes on. Anyway, we went down and dad made us lie down, and it was in that raid that we had it.'

Just before the bomb dropped on Milton Avenue her father, as he was leaving the house, 'saw a plane coming at him. He could see the pilot in the light of the fires – they were machine-gunning':

'You could hear the zoom of the planes diving and the whine of their engines. Then, all of a sudden dad fell down on my mum and he said, "Oh my gosh!" You didn't hear your bomb. It shook like this then down came all the stuff on us. We didn't know what the time was or anything else. And dad called out to us, "Are you all right Pam? Are you all right Elsie?" We both said yes. We couldn't feel each other or do anything. Well, the only thing with me was I was caught across my back on something and I couldn't move my legs down – mind,

I had no shoes on my feet. So, anyway, we were there for ages and we got soaking wet – a water pipe must have burst somewhere.'

'From what appeared to be a long way away they could hear somebody shouting, "Percy! Percy! Anybody down there?" Percy shouted up, but nobody heard him. Then they heard a tapping noise and Elsie said, "Oh, that's somebody trying to get to us!" Being in a dazed and confused state, and not realising what had happened, she thought it was somebody at the front door. Mr and Mrs Kingston (their neighbours) knew that the Taylor family had been in the house that night, and so digging began. It took the rescuers between eight and ten hours to release the Taylors from the rubble.

Percy was the first to be got out, then Elsie, and finally Pamela, who thought 'it was a miracle' that she was saved. 'I could get myself through the hole and I went right across that place without cutting my feet!' The rescue services took them to St Martin's Hospital 'in some sort of army truck and you had to lay on hard stuff. I sat up in the front with the driver.' As they were going down Milton Avenue, Pamela saw her grandfather coming up. She asked the driver to stop, but he couldn't because he had somebody onboard from Shakespeare Avenue who was very badly injured. On arrival at St Martin's:

'All the soldiers, the wounded, had got up out of their beds for us, but I didn't want a bed. They put mum and dad to bed. They

All that remained of the Taylor's home after it was struck by a high explosive bomb at about 5.15am on 26 April.

The scene of devastation after the first two raids, looking down the lower end of King Edward Road towards Third Avenue.

This is the same view today (below right) with homes rebuilt, showing few signs of the scars from the Blitz.

gave us some drinks. My mum was getting worried about her mum and dad who lived in the Wellsway, so I said I'd walk down.

'But did I have a job! They had an unexploded bomb somewhere between Devonshire Buildings and the top of Wellsway, so I had to come down Entry Hill where there were houses with all the glass out. I got down to the bottom and found my grandma.'

After doing his duty during the night, Ray Burgess left the fire station at Cleveland Bridge early on the Sunday morning and made for home on his motorbike. When he reached King Edward Road, he found that 'there was chaos everywhere – you couldn't stay on the bike for long because of the debris'.

Coming off fire-watching duty at the Abbey, Freda Beatty made her way down Southgate Street towards the Old Bridge. She intended taking the quick route home by going up Holloway, but was met by two wardens, one of whom said, 'Will you go round the other way, by the station, we've got a couple of little babies here that we don't want to disturb.' They were referring, of course, to two unexploded bombs in the region St James's Street.

On Sunday morning, John Coe and his schoolmates walked as usual from their school on Widcombe Hill to the service at St James's church at Southgate. Once they had reached the city centre, they had to 'pick their way through the bomb-ravaged streets'. During the service 'the vicar, the Reverend Martin Colbourn, sang a solo from the pulpit, a massive structure, which moved across the front of the church on brass rails. We were unaware that bodies from the bombing were laid out in the crypt below the church, and that within a few hours, the building itself would be wrecked when the bombers returned.'

Bob White, who lived at 4 Milton Avenue, helped a Civil Defence squad from Bristol collect bodies from Bath's streets and take them to the city mortuary on the Sunday morning.
(*Bob White*)

By 1942, Aubrey Jackman was serving in the Army. April of that year found him setting up a tented camp at the Marquis of Bristol's park near Bury St Edmunds. As soon as news of the first Blitz reached him, he was given compassionate leave and he returned to Bath. Upon going straight to the Lansdown Grove Hotel where his mother was living, he found that 'every window had been blown out – a bomb having landed on the Bath High School immediately opposite'. According to Dr Ted Matthews, 'the bomb had dropped right in the middle of the big tree going from the laboratory to the gym, and blew it right out of the ground'. The gym disappeared completely.

On the Sunday morning, clearing up began in the city. Frank Mawer with other members of the Home Guard helped to clear up in the Kingsmead Square area. He remembers that near Abbey Church House there was a line of shops including a wine and spirit merchants, and they came across a lot of unopened bottles but were told to leave them alone! In that area there was a curious incident:

> 'A woman had been killed, and her husband, who couldn't be found, was eventually discovered on the seat on the way to Abbey Church House. He had been blown there from his house.

> There was a lot of clearing up to do – it wasn't nice. There was a lot of dust and dirt, and that sort of thing. You got an idea if there was anybody there. Fortunately, I didn't come too close to it.'

Bob White and his father decided they ought to report to their respective Home Guard companies for duty. Bob recalls:

> 'I went down to the headquarters and was immediately assigned to some Civil Defence from Bristol who were going round picking up bodies. I spent all morning going round [the city] showing them where these various places were. We didn't actually help them [to move the bodies] because most of the ones that were dead had been laid out and they were just picked up and taken to the mortuary. It was very strange. I was young and I don't really think it sunk in.'

However, there was one bomb incident that Bob attended with the Civil Defence team on that Sunday morning which touched a nerve:

> 'I can remember one very sad one up at Bloomfield Drive. They lived in a house that had a very long garden – I'd think about 100 yards long, with a shelter down at the bottom. They had all disappeared down to the shelter. It was a lady with one child whose husband was in the RAF and he happened to be home on leave and they'd all gone into the shelter and it got a direct hit. The house was untouched. That was terribly sad.'

The family who perished were Frank Brown, a 31-year-old RAF flight sergeant, his wife Beatrice (29) and their 4-year-old daughter Margaret. Originally from south-east London, it was a bitter twist of fate that they should meet their ends in a 'safe' provincial city, far from the dangers and devastation of the capital.

Meanwhile, 'Rocky' Rochester had been running messages all night between the Twerton Roundhill Wardens' Post and Civil Defence Control at Apsley House in Newbridge Hill. 'Rocky' had finally completed his duties at lunchtime on the Sunday. His description of the aftermath of the last two raids in his own neighbourhood brings home something of the awful cost in human lives.

> 'I had a look at the local damage in my area of Roundhill Park. The road I cycled down had a bomb crater in it and several houses were damaged, the side entrance into Roundhill Park also had a crater. A house on the left-hand corner had been demolished, but also caught on fire. The charred remains of a mother and daughter were in a bath

on the path. It looked a heap of brown flesh with a bone showing. I can still see it because it was so white. A dog was gnawing at it and I drove it away. A damaged bungalow, almost opposite in The Hollow, was also sad. I looked around the wreckage and on entering the bedroom I found an old couple laying side by side in bed, dead, with badly bruised faces. A concrete lintel had landed across their heads.'

Ivor Barnsdale was billeted with the Falconer family in Brunswick Place at the time of the Blitz:

'After a frightful Saturday night, Bath was in chaos. Most traffic was diverted via Widcombe and Pulteney Road to North Parade and Pulteney Street, or Bathwick Street. I spent from about 10am to 6pm, clad in grew flannels and an open neck shirt, directing traffic at the junction of North Parade and Pulteney Road. Then, after calling in at Brunswick Place, I went to Ensleigh on fire-watching duty, which consisted largely of putting out small incendiary devices as they landed on concrete roofs, and later, after the third raid, watching the Assembly Rooms go up in flames.'

Eileen Wiggins (Grace Selley's sister) remembers that on Sunday morning she walked over to Charlcombe to see if her in-laws were alright:

'And then I went back to Oldfield Park to see if my husband's gran was OK. And then I went back to Caledonian Road, and I only got as far as Stuart Place and there was a policeman walking along, and he wanted to know what I was doing. And I said I'd come to see if my gran was all right at 44. And he said, "Everybody's out of here, they've all had to be moved out because of these bombs." But I went round the back, and there was poor gran – she wasn't really with us. And I said to the policeman, "Well, I've got to take her over to Walcot, home." And he said, "How will you do that?" And I said, "Oh, I'll go up to Junction Road, there's a taxi place – there's a garage up there." And meanwhile, the postman very kindly picked up a couple of blankets and things, and put her in a wheel chair and pushed her up the back garden and along to Brook Road, and then I come down over the bridge and we went out to Walcot. I just picked up a few bits and pieces in a suitcase, and the back door was off, and that was it.

'Going along in the Paragon there was a great big gap where old Dr Middlemas [lived] – she'd been out all night, and she'd come back to have, well, I suppose a rest and a cup of coffee, and they were killed with a direct hit. And my father worked at the ice factory down in Walcot Street ... and all that rubble had come down into Walcot

Street. He'd decided he'd better go into Broad Street and see if his family were all right, and poor old dad was left there all on his own.'

Phyllis and Arnold Miles walked down to Fortt's in Milsom Street for Sunday lunch 'because we had no gas or water. We got there a bit late. We heard there had been a real slap-up lunch laid on but were a bit late arriving, so had to make do with corned beef and mash.' Aubrey Jackman remembers that 'the maximum meal charge in restaurants, Fortt's and the Old Red House, and hotels was five shillings [25p]'.

Eileen Rogers knew that her father would have to go back into town again, and she was concerned that the bombers would come again that Sunday night:

'Some friends of ours (the average family didn't have a telephone in those days) at Southdown, we were in touch with them, were going out Englishcombe way and not staying in Bath overnight. So we joined them, and when I think about it, it was like a lot of refugees. They were coming up Coronation Avenue and we came from Englishcombe Lane, and we all trekked down over Padleigh to get to Priston.

'We found a field that had a large ditch, and we all thought it looked quite safe, and it had trees along it. So, our friends, my family and several others, all got down into this long gully thing and bedded down there for the night. It was a moonlit night. We were not prepared, but it was dry of course. It was a beautiful night, and what was referred to in wartime as a "bomber's moon". It was just as frightening, but at least you knew there was not a house to fall on top of you. If you were going to be killed, it was to be in the ditch! Some people for whom there wasn't enough room in this gully were sheltering in the end of the hedge in the field just up above.

'As soon as the sirens went the planes came over, and although we were actually out in the countryside, we saw them go over the trees – we could actually see them, damn great big black shapes coming so low, they were very low, and it was horrible. These people started running and panicked, and then they all ran down towards the gully.

'With some fires still burning in Bath, that night the bombers didn't really need directions – they were able to pick the city out and bomb again. And, of course, when the "all-clear" finally went, we all got up and shook ourselves down. Then there was the trek back home, where you just didn't know what you were going back to. You didn't know whether your house would still be standing. But our concern was for my father

Over 400 people lost their lives during the Baedeker Blitz on Bath. They included civilians, Civil Defence workers, Home Guard personnel, and servicemen and women who were staying in the city during that fateful weekend. While many were interred in two mass graves at Haycombe Cemetery, others were laid to rest elsewhere in the city and beyond. These headstones in St Michael's Cemetery are inscribed with the names of Private F.J. Park (17), and Private A.R. Woods (19), two gallant young members of the 5th Somerset (Bath City) Battalion, Home Guard, who sacrificed their lives for others during the raids on 26 April 1942.

Boys in the Blitz: Scout Patrol Leader Leslie Hawkins, 17th Bath (1st Walcot) Troop, received the Scout Gilt Cross for his gallantry in 'rescuing, in the face of danger, persons trapped in the wreckage of their homes during the raids'. Scout G.A. Wall, 21st Bath (Victoria Hall) Troop, Larkhall, received the Certificate of Gallantry in recognition of his valuable assistance to the police as a messenger. The awards were made at the Pump Room on 14 November 1942.

who had been in Bath during the bombing, and if he would be coming home. As we got towards Englishcombe Lane, a policeman was coming off duty who had been on all night, and he was able to tell us that dad was alright, so that was a big relief to us.

'The house was alright, apart from the front door that seemed to have come off its hinges, and we couldn't close it properly. You could tell that there had been an air-raid. The smell of the fires seemed to hang over everything. We were terrified what was going to happen next. They were bound to come back again on the Monday night.'

Having done her fire-watching duty at the Abbey on the Saturday night, Freda Beatty spent the Sunday night at Englishcombe Lane with Leslie and Enid Bell with whom she was lodging. Mr Bell, Headmaster of Weymouth House School, had built a shelter in the living room of the house, and that is where the three of them took shelter during the third raid.

Fearful of the bombers returning on the Sunday night, Phyllis Bond decided to sleep at her sister's home:

'This time my mother-in-law and sister-in-law as well, trekked over to Broadmoor Park. A good job we did because Jerry came that night to finish off anything he'd left standing the night before. My in-laws had a few broken windows but nothing much else, so they could go back home. We were not allowed back to Albany Road, except to collect a few essentials like clothes, until the Army sent somebody to defuse the time bomb. During this time I slipped back into the street one dinner time to collect

letters my husband had sent (he was in the Army serving in Burma).
I was in trouble with the police for doing this, but they let me through.'

In spite of their arduous work during the first two raids, Allan Woods called for his friend Fred Park on the Sunday evening to go on firewatching duty at the premises of Norton Dairies in Circus Mews, near Margaret's Buildings, where Allan also worked as a motor maintenance engineer. Fred's sister Kathleen begged him not to go, but he insisted, saying it was his duty. When the sirens went at 1.15am on Monday morning heralding the third raid, Fred returned home briefly during the raid to check that his mother and sisters were safe. They had taken refuge beneath their kitchen table. Fred returned to his firewatching duties at Norton Dairies shortly before the building received a direct hit. Both Fred and Allan were killed. They died together doing their duty and were buried together at St Michael's cemetery.

Allan's boss at Norton Dairies was Leonard Smith, the head motor maintenance engineer, who was also a part-time volunteer fireman

This large crater in the centre of the Circus was made by the bomb that killed Fireman Leonard Smith. It is seen from a house in the east segment not long after the raids. In front of the houses in the north segment can be seen a hoist positioned to remove another unexploded bomb. Dr Sammy Marle wrote on 8 May, 'an enormous crater in the green. More craters & unexploded stuff by No. 3 and in front of No. 14 – they have got that out today.' (*From a watercolour by Norma Bull, courtesy of Victoria Art Gallery, Bath*)

in the AFS. Tragically, Leonard had died some 24 hours before Allan, in the second raid on Sunday morning. He was on duty in the Circus when a bomb that had fallen in the grass in the centre, where it had lain unexploded, blew up and killed him when the Fire Service started up a pump nearby. For three days he was missing and his wife and two daughters suffered dreadfully waiting for news. Finally, the manager of Norton Dairies visited all the city mortuaries in an effort to discover his fate. Eventually, he was identified by his fireman's uniform – shortly before he was due to be buried as an unknown casualty in the mass communal grave at Haycombe Cemetery. He was later buried with full honours from the Fire Service. Leonard was the only firefighter to die in the raids and his loss, together with that of Allan Woods, the dairy's two motor engineers, must have brought chaos as well as sadness to the firm.

Bob White remembers that at about 9 o'clock on the Sunday evening, one of the billetees who was staying with his family at their home in Milton Avenue, came down stairs and said to them:

'"I think they're coming again tonight." I think he must have had some knowledge. I don't know how he knew this, I hadn't an inkling. "We'll go out in the car, we won't stay in Bath", he said to us. All four of us got in the car and drove out to Timsbury and we just settled down in the car and dozed off. He said, "Well, we'll see. If they don't come by 12 o'clock we'll go back and we'll just have a snooze".

' 12 o'clock came and nothing had happened so we drove back into Bath and we were just driving up Milton Avenue when the siren went. He did the quickest reverse I've ever seen back up Wellsway. And as we went along the top by Fuller's Earth we could actually see the bombers coming over, they were so low. We disappeared a bit farther out and we could hear all the bombs dropping.'

Ted Peters was 12 years old and lived with his family at 10 Kingsmead West flats, near to the river. Fearful of the bombers returning again on the Sunday night, Ted's father Robert decided they wouldn't stay around to greet them. Instead, the family sought shelter in a barn at Claverton Down. Ted's most vivid memory of the Blitz was 'looking down on the city and it was as though someone had filled a swimming bath full of petrol and lit it, and I thought then that dad was right bringing us up here. How anyone could live through that I'll never know.'

R.C. Fry recalls standing in the garden of her brother-in-law's cottage up at Foxhill before daybreak on the Sunday morning, 'overlooking the whole of the valley in which Bath lies, watching the horrifying sight of bombers coming over and releasing their load and seeing the resulting explosions and fires'.

Muriel Elmes, who had been teaching in Birmingham, returned to Bath in 1941 after an absence of 10 years, to teach at West Twerton Secondary Modern School in The Hollow. She was at the school in the fateful early hours of Monday morning, 27 April, with Mr R.O. Dann, the Headmaster (who was also a Special Constable and ARP Warden), Miss Lawrence, Miss Dorothy Benjafield, Mr George Babington (also an Auxiliary Fireman), and another member of staff.

> 'The school had been turned into a rest and feeding centre, and some 200 people from the area of The Hollow had come along. We knew exactly when the bomb hit the school – every electric clock stopped dead at 10 minutes to 2. Many people were killed, many injured – we never knew exactly how many. Ambulances arrived, taking the injured to the hospitals. My home was not damaged the night the school was hit.'

 This photograph was taken during the Blitz weekend by Eric Lanning from his home at 9 Cavendish Crescent. Doric House, the home of Miss Consuelo De Reyes and her husband Peter King, can be seen smouldering after an incendiary bomb set fire to part of the house. The first bomb to be dropped on Bath, several years earlier, landed in the allotments on the High Common. The crater that resulted can be seen at the top left of the picture. (*Eric Lanning*)

BLITZ WEEKEND

After going home and getting some sleep, Muriel awoke about 5am:

'There was a rumbling noise, as if a plane was in difficulty, so I went outside to investigate. As I reached the corner of the back wall of the bungalow I looked up – the plane was not much above rooftop level. Next, I spotted the swastika, and then found myself looking straight at the rear gunner. I disappeared very quickly. Nothing happened for a few moments, then another gunner spattered the road ahead with bullets – just to let off steam, I suppose.'

Following the bombing of West Twerton School, Joan Potter and her fellow pupils were transferred to West Central School, whose pupils in turn were moved either to the City of Bath Girls' School or the Technical College, where Joan was sent:

'Our lessons were held around the city in different buildings, and so we spent a lot of time walking from one place to another. Some lessons were held at Weymouth House School, Millbrook School, and the College in Beau Street. For maths I had to go to the Old Gaol in Oldfield Park. For games we had to make our own way to the Glasshouse playing fields on Combe Down.'

 A dramatic photograph of St James's church burning in the early hours of Monday 27 April, seen from Lower Borough Walls. After the previous night's bombing, during which the church escaped unscathed, the crypt had been pressed into service as a temporary mortuary.

That Sunday night, Dr Sammy Marle had gone to bed dressed ready for immediate action in his Home Guard uniform. The siren went at about 1.30am and when he went outside he found 'the whole countryside around ... ablaze with incendiaries':

'We hadn't heard any come down, though Hun planes had been over and over. By the grace of Heaven none were on the house. I put one out just over the fence and then stood by hoping the Hun would not lash at us with his HEs [High Explosives]. He machine-gunned rather wildly round about, and then apparently two houses caught fire in Sion Road, for he had concentrated down there. In all, eight were burnt out including the one where old Kynevin was billeted. He was in the basement with two maids, and they were lucky to make their escape through a small fanlight, much too small for Kynevin! I passed down the road to the RUH by car just after they had crept out and he looked somewhat shattered. "Look where I got out", he said. And, by heavens, I wonder he did! There were fires in Cavendish Place and people were dashing in and out of their houses with furniture and things.

'In the early hours before going off, I took Patch and Marian [his dogs] for a walk over John Levis' field to see the fires raging in the city. It looked as if the Empire Hotel, St James' church and all that area was well alight. The Circus was, or seemed to be blazing. We had done so much the previous day at the RUH that no more was possible for an hour or two, so I went round to the Butchers', Cuppages', Church Street home where they were singed with fire and a Sister was buried in the flat across the road. And so on to the Circus where I found John Bastow's and the next house burnt out, my house evacuated, Kindersley's too. An enormous crater in the green [centre of the Circus]. More craters and unexploded stuff by No 3, and in front of No 14. (They have got that out today [8 May] only.) Altogether a scene of appalling disorder and destruction. Yet everyone getting about his job quite calmly and efficiently. Firemen and hoses everywhere. Traffic controlled by Home Guard – rescue parties hard at work – and altogether a jolly picnic.'

'Hitler thought he was going to frighten me, but he was wrong. I defied him and am still alive!' Mrs Elizabeth Vick, aged 101, was evacuated from her home at 7 Belvedere, Lansdown Road, to the Aikman Eventide Home on Bathwick Hill during one of the raids.

At some time on the Sunday, Frank Mawer heard that they'd 'better be prepared for something' that night. So, Dudu and Pam's landlady at Great Bedford Street allowed Pam's boyfriend and Frank to stay with the girls, but 'no "hanky-panky", mind you!' When the siren went they all trooped down to the cellars. Sometime later they heard the whistle of a bomb quite near and decided to leave the house. On emerging they found fires all around them. A house opposite was 'blazing merrily' and Frank admitted that he'd never been so frightened as he was that night.

 Top: Damaged homes in Lower Oldfield Park and the rubble that used to be the Medical Centre at No 110 after it received a direct hit. Neighbouring properties suffered from the blast and the effects of shrapnel and flying debris. In the foreground, firemen's hoses can be seen snaking along the road. Above: The same view in 2021. No 110 was rebuilt in 1948, but unlike the repairs to adjacent properties it was not reinstated in the same architectural style.

Not far away in Brunswick Place, at regular intervals during the raid Jack Falconer, accompanied by David, his eight-year-old son, went upstairs from the hall where he and others were sheltering to check the roof for incendiary bombs. David remembers that the ceiling of one of the upstairs bedrooms at the back of the house was a vivid red – a reflection of the fire at the Assembly Rooms just below. He also saw fires raging all over the city.

Meanwhile, Dudu, Pam, Frank and Pam's boyfriend went up Park Street and turned left to the High Common, where Pam got a telephone wire wrapped around her neck – a bomb had brought the wires down. Once on the Common 'we were attacked. I don't suppose they really saw us,' Frank recalled, 'they saw a group of people, but it looked as though they were really going for us because we could see the tracers coming out of the plane.'

From the High Common they moved towards the fields above Weston village where a farmer allowed them to shelter in one of his barns. From there they walked to somewhere in the Newbridge area and eventually they came to a big house 'where the maids were still in uniform'. Having been invited in they found about 40 other people there. They were given coffee and biscuits 'and food of one kind or another'. They left the house in the early morning and made their way to Frank's billet in Bathwick Street where they had a quick wash. After the girls had left, Frank had a message to report in uniform to his Home Guard company.

> 'Our little squad of 32 were promptly marched out to the bottom of Victoria Park, and from there to somewhere beyond the gasworks. We were led by our hastily marching lieutenant, who had never been known to march so quickly. "Why are you going so quickly?" we asked him. "We shall get there!" "Well," he said, "you see that barrel down there ... that's an unexploded bomb".'

When the 'all-clear' sounded at 2.05am early on the Monday morning after the third and final heavy raid of the Bath Blitz, nearly 400 men, women and children lay dead. Many hundreds more were injured, filling the wards of the city's hospitals. Whole families had been wiped out and complete communities devastated. If anything, the German bomber crews who visited Bath that weekend had not discriminated on grounds of wealth or social standing, much to the contrary. No particular social class, profession or trade had been spared their evil attentions – among those killed were aristocrats, clergymen, doctors and civil servants, as well as the poorest working-class men, women and children.

Shrapnel damage to the masonry of No 101 Lower Oldfield Park, on the opposite side of the road to No 110, is still evident in 2021.

The following statistics of the raids speak for themselves: more than one-third of those who died were of middle age, but over one-fifth of the dead were young people under the age of 21. Over half of the city's dead were female. More than a quarter (over 100) of the Blitz victims who were buried in the communal graves at Haycombe cemetery were not identified.

Material destruction of the city was severe, with some 19,000 buildings destroyed or damaged due to bombing. Such widespread demolition of property by high explosive and incendiary was to have a far-reaching effect upon Bath's urban renewal in the postwar years, when the misguided vision of city planners completed what the German Luftwaffe had begun.

CHAPTER 5
BLITZ – THE AFTERMATH

On Monday morning, as the first shafts of daylight broke the grip of a second night of horror, people all over Bath looked out across their smoke-wreathed, smouldering city. Peeping from their dank shelters or staring through glassless windows, they bore witness to grotesque scenes of death and destruction. From the back garden of their school in Widcombe Hill, John Coe and his schoolmates surveyed the scene of desolation. They could dimly decipher the large letters on the Evans & Owen sign in Bartlett Street against clouds of smoke issuing from the still burning Assembly Rooms and St Andrew's church beyond.

 Rivers Street photographed in 2021 from the same viewpoint as the picture opposite that was taken in 1942. The absence of St Andrew's church with its tall spire is probably the most striking feature.

Down in the city that had been brought to the brink of social collapse, half-desperate attempts were made to maintain some element of normality. Individuals struggled to behave as if it was business as usual – making a pot of tea or sweeping the front step (even if it had been demolished in the bombing) helped people to cope with the massive upheaval that had been foisted on them. But the shock of the raids caused some people to react in peculiar ways, as Christina Brooks recalls. 'One of my mother's friends stood outside her bombed and burning house and cried hysterically because she could not rescue her fur coat.'

When officials from the Ministry of Home Security visited Bath in the aftermath of the raids, they were very critical of the city's Civil Defence response to the bombing. The Civil Defence Control Centre at Apsley House on Newbridge Road had been evacuated on the Sunday morning after communications were cut off by the bombing, moving across the city to the back-up centre in the Forester's Arms at Combe Down. An official report observed that conditions at the Forester's were chaotic and concluded that the authorities had been operating very close to the limit of their capacity.

High above Bath and unseen from the ground, a lone RAF Spitfire from No 1 Photo Reconnaissance Unit was photographing the city. It had taken off in the early afternoon from Benson in Oxfordshire to make a record of the bomb damage. Normally, the unit's task was to photograph cities in occupied Europe to assess results after Bomber Command had visited them, only this time it was photographing an English city after the

St Andrew's church soon after the raid in which it was burned out by incendiary bombs. Jack Falconer, in light coloured raincoat and flat cap, stands talking to another man on Rivers Street.

Bath after the Blitz, or a bomber's-eye view. Aerial reconnaissance photographs of the undefended city were taken on Monday 27 April 1942 by an RAF Spitfire from No 1 Photo Reconnaissance Unit.

Luftwaffe had called. The high-level coverage from about 30,000ft shows veils of smoke obscuring neighbourhoods like Cheltenham Street and Westmoreland Street on the Lower Bristol Road, while north of the river St Andrew's church and buildings on Julian Road are still smouldering.

Walking near the Somerset & Dorset railway line that ran along the bottom of Lymore Gardens in Oldfield Park, Keith Gover saw that bodies of Blitz victims from Millmead Road had been laid out in a small garage. And later as he passed the cemetery in the Lower Bristol Road, he was horrified to see bodies everywhere; it was hard to tell whether they had been killed recently or were corpses blown out of their graves by the bombing.

All across the city, hordes of labourers from the Engineer's Department armed with shovels had begun the back-breaking task of removing tons of broken glass from Bath's roads, avenues and streets and loading it on to carts and wagons. Seen through the smoke-tinged dawn light, the shining heaps gave the appearance of mounds of accumulated ice. The job would take them the better part of a week to complete. In the days that followed, a small army of almost 3,000 building tradesmen was rapidly assembled and soon was hard at work repairing shattered roofs and windows.

Rescue Squads at work in the rubble of what had been Victoria Road at the top of Brougham Hayes. Ten people died in the second attack when a direct hit by a 1,000kg bomb on No 3 caused 21 other houses to be destroyed and 36 more damaged.

Civil Defence rescue parties toiled day and night to extract victims of the bombing who were still alive, but trapped beneath their wrecked homes. There was also the unpleasant job of recovering the bodies of those who had been killed and whose corpses remained buried

beneath tons of fallen masonry. On 1 May, the *Chronicle* reported the recovery of the body of Dr Mary Middlemass from what was left of her home on the Paragon:

'When, on Wednesday [30 April], after ceaseless digging, a rescue squad party recovered her body, she was found wearing her fur coat and tin helmet, just ready to go out to her post. Her sisters Elsie and Jean were lying near her, also dead, together with Dr Mary's two maids, Miss Enid Hawkins [24] and Miss Freda Baker [17].'

The Middlemass sisters were from Rennington in Northumberland and established themselves in professional careers at a time when the campaign for women's suffrage was reaching its peak in Britain. Their father, Edward, was a blacksmith who, with his wife Robina, believed in the importance of education for their seven children. Dr Mary, MB, ChB, who was 42, studied medicine at Edinburgh. After qualifying in 1921, she held posts as House Surgeon at Macclesfield General Infirmary and the Children's Hospital, Sheffield. Dr Mary went to Bath in 1924 and built up a large practice. She was Medical Officer to the Waifs and Strays Home at Box and to the Home Office School, Avonside School for Girls, Bath. In 1939, Dr Mary helped set up the First Aid Post at Snow Hill where she gave classes and demonstrations each week so that her staff had a really first-class training. Her sister Jean (46), a teacher of history at South Shields, was about to take up the headship of Brampton Girls Secondary School in September 1942. Elsie (39) was a chartered physiotherapist. She had served in the First World War, was a former head of the physiotherapy department at Bath and Wessex Children's Orthopaedic Hospital (1929–36), and a volunteer Civil Defence ambulance driver based at the Snow Hill First Aid Post.

 All that remained of the home of Dr Mary Middlemass at 29 The Paragon. She and her sister Elsie had returned for a brief respite from duty during the third raid when the house was struck by a high explosive bomb that killed both women, their elder sister Jean who was visiting, and their two maids.

A happier story of a successful rescue was also reported in the same edition:

'A Bath family of seven have been rescued unharmed from the Morrison indoor shelter on to which their three-storied house collapsed during Saturday's raid. Neighbours and Civil Defence workers saw a light coming from the rubble. They dug down, found the shelter, cut with pliers the protecting wire "walls" and brought the family to safety.'

BLITZ - THE AFTERMATH

A rare photograph of Dr Mary Middlemass.

Bath Civil Defence Casualty Service's Kensington Ambulance and First Aid Depot, under the supervision of Drs A. Evans, Hugh Smith and R. Mortimer (pictured front row in 'civvies'). Miss Elsie Middlemass, younger sister of Dr Mary Middlemass, is in the front row fourth from the right. (*David Crellin*)

Eileen Wiggins found that attempts to return to normality were not easy to achieve. Mr Dolman, the undertaker, her next-door neighbour, had spent all Sunday night at the mortuary beneath the railway arches near the Old Bridge. On his return home at 8 o'clock on the Monday morning, Mr Dolman banged on Eileen's door and found the family half-asleep. He told them that the first five houses were 'down' in Hanover Terrace where they had relations living, and that somebody ought to go up to see if they were safe. Having made everyone a cup of tea, Eileen then decided that although she should have been at work, she had better go to Hanover Terrace.

> 'Anyway, I goes up over Snow Hill – there were boulders everywhere, and burst pipes and gas mains. And when I got to the bottom of Hanover Terrace there was an ARP man there, and he said, "you can't go up there my dear". I said, "Well, I'm going up to see about a family I know".'

As she reached Hanover Terrace, Eileen saw that the first five houses had indeed been demolished. Window frames and glass had been blown out. It was a windy morning and some of the frames 'was a-blowing in the wind'. From No 5 upwards, all the front doors had been blown out and were lying on the steps, and there was water everywhere:

These brick and concrete surface shelters in Cheltenham Street survived the bombing of nearby houses.

'Anyway, we crossed the road to the other side and we picked our way to No 12, moved the door and I went in and called my aunt. "Oh, and am I glad to see you!" She was trying to make a cup of tea on a primus stove. She had two children: one was nearly six and the other eight. They were both asleep on mattresses. And all of a sudden I heard a little chuckle, and in the corner there was this little 11-month-old child. The soot – I'm not exaggerating – that had come down the chimney, was just like a mountain, all in the room, and she was like a little picaninny, and there she was, sat there in the chair, and you knew, she put her arms out to me. She was as black as a tinker, she really was! And I picked her up by the armpits and I carried her through all this rubble down home. And she [her aunt] said, "When the children wake up, I'll bring them down". And then I had another cup of tea and a wash and I put them to bed, and I thought, I ought to go to work!'

Since the beginning of the war, Eileen had been 'doing her bit' at the Co-op in Widcombe Parade where she packed cheese and margarine. Realising that she had spent a considerable time with her relations, Eileen:

'... more or less raced all down St John's Road, under the archway, all along the river bank and in the back of the Co-op. And a voice called out, "Who's that down there?" And I said, "It's me. I'm sorry I'm late." He said, "Everybody's late! You can't come in this way." The back warehouse had a glass roof, and the glass and the stuff went over everything. Someone had been round and boarded up the front door and there was, you know; the usual people banging on the door for their rations – I mean, we just couldn't sell anything until it had all been sorted out, you know.'

Joan Barlow and her Admiralty colleagues returned to work in their offices at The Royal School as usual. At lunchtime, they decided to go into Bath as they had heard that 'all the restaurants had to serve British restaurant meals at very cheap prices'. They were surprised to find that some of the food they were served had not been available in the shops since the start of the war. The following week, the *Chronicle* announced that, in the wake of the Blitz:

> 'It was reported to the Bath Emergency Committee on Friday that 30,000 meals a day (including snacks) were being served and that the service was expanding continually. Efforts are being made to obtain 100 paid helpers.'

For another young woman, whose circumstances were less fortunate than Joan Barlow's, Providence smiled on her in a different way. Kathleen Seers, who had lost her home in the Blitz, was a shorthand typist at the Children's Orthopaedic Hospital. She and her mother realised they were very lucky that it was only their home they had lost and not their lives – their house at 23 Magdalen Avenue was the only one bombed in the avenue of forty-five dwellings.

> 'The hospital had wonderful benefactors – the Wills family, of tobacco fame. On the Monday after the bombing, Mrs Wills rang the hospital to offer temporary accommodation to any member of the staff who had been made homeless. I was the only one. Her chauffeur picked us up in the afternoon and took us to the beautiful family home, Hamswell House, which is situated between Bath and Bristol. Mrs Wills was a lovely lady and we were treated as equals despite the fact that we only had the clothes we stood in and were very grubby as well!'

It was not long before word of Bath's plight had spread across the nation. From all over the country gifts of clothing for bombed-out homeless people who had lost everything began pouring in to Bath clothing depot. 'Everybody has been incredibly kind. The response has been splendid, and it seems that people must almost have robbed their own backs to send the clothing', remarked a WVS worker. At the rest centres clothing was issued to those who only had what they stood up in when they arrived.

David Falconer, who spent both nights of the Blitz at home in Brunswick Place, remembers having to queue up for water with a large jug outside the barber's shop, which occupied the same premises as the newsagent in Julian Road. For some reason the water supply there was still on. The plate glass window had been blown out, and people had to step through the open window frame to fill their receptacles.

After enduring the first night's bombing at nearby Morford Street, the Miles's had decided to take shelter on the Sunday night under the arches beneath Camden Crescent where they stayed until the third raid was over:

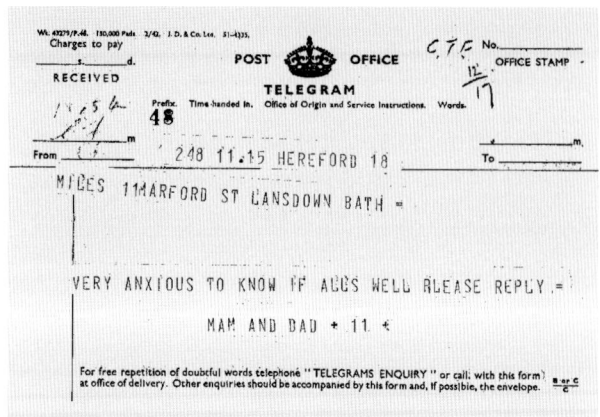

Arnold and Phyllis Miles were living in a flat on Morford Street during the Blitz. News of the raids soon spread and relatives were anxious to know their loved ones were safe. The Miles's received this Post Office telegram from Arnold's parents in Herefordshire. (*Arnold and Phyllis Miles*)

'On the Monday morning after the raid the air smelled acrid, it was horrible. You could smell the burning that had been going on. It was on the Sunday night that the Assembly Rooms had been hit and that was my first really emotional time to see it going up in flames. They used it for a food store where a lot of tinned fruit had been stored. You could hear all those tins popping in the fire. My husband went further afield than I did and saw some horrific sights. I remember that the buses were few and far between because there were so many craters in the roads. Some firms put on transport for those workers who couldn't get to work. We couldn't get out of Bath for quite a time by train after the Blitz. My parents sent us a telegram enquiring whether we were safe or not. We couldn't get a reply back to them, so that was pretty harrowing.'

However, the authorities were only too aware of the vital need to keep lines of communication open in order to avoid rumours spreading. 'Mobile PO vans' valuable work at Bath' headlined the *Chronicle* on 9 May:

'Nearly 500 telegrams were dealt with every day by a staff of two in each of two mobile post offices, which arrived on the morning following the second Blitz on Bath [Monday]. They were open at nine o'clock in the morning to issue postage stamps and accept mail. Army pensions and allowances, and old age pensions were also dealt with. The telegraph section was the busiest with people sending wires to relations. Between 400 and 500 were sent from each of the offices on the first three days of last week

Among the many emergency services that went into action following the Blitz were mobile laundries.

after which one of the vans was withdrawn to another area.'

Other, non-governmental, agencies also played a valuable part in helping the city return to a semblance of normality. For Margaret Haynes, a student teacher at Bristol University, the image of the dazed and ravaged city of Bath made a lasting impression on her young mind. She was one of a group of undergraduates who visited Bath on the Monday after the raids as part of a relief effort organised by the university.

WE ARE OPEN

Our Glass has gone but our stock is intact— We Are, As Usual **At Your Service**

CECIL LTD. **WALKER**
ONE, THE CORRIDOR, BATH
And at Weston-super-Mare
'Phone: BATH 4540. W.-S.-M. 418.

The British are a stoical people and during all the deprivation and horror of the war years they just 'got on with it'. Cecil Walker Ltd was typical of Bath's shops and its citizens in the days after the Blitz: life quickly returned to normal with 'business as usual'.

'We were taken over to Bath on a bus with our bicycles so that we could act as emergency message carriers. Bath was inundated with telegrams and who could deliver them? Call out the students! We cycled all over Bath carrying and bringing back reports. It was heart-breaking. We would go to an address only to find that it wasn't there anymore.

'I cycled out to one address and found the lady of the house in labour. The neighbour ladies [sic] were there to answer the door. The air-raid warden in charge of one message delivery operation laughed at the report I wrote: "Lady of the house in labour. No damage."

'I shall never forget the streets of Bath all crunchy with broken glass and rubble. The shocked, tense faces of the people and this stiff upper-lip thing that kept them from crying and raging over the loss and the desolation. Why didn't they weep and mourn and lament? It would have been much better for everybody.'

On that Monday morning, Dr Sammy Marle noted that both the Regina Hotel at the bottom of Russell Street and the (continued on page 102)

A sea of rubble in Cheltenham Street off the Lower Bristol Road is all that remains of people's homes. In the centre of the picture, just in front of the houses, can be seen three brick-built street shelters that also appear on page 94. Miraculously, they survived the bombing and protected their occupants from death and injury. At top left is the water tower alongside the GWR main railway line.

Debris has been cleared from Railway Road (centre, with parked cars). The tall chimney belongs to the Cooperative Dairy in Dorchester Street and in the background (with three chimneys) is the electricity generating station, demolished to make way for today's city bus station.

  Julian Road looking east towards Harley Street and St Mary's church and (below) the burnt-out ruin of St Andrew's church, looking west, with Northampton Street on the right. These photographs taken a year or so after the raids show that little had been done to make good the damage other than clearing rubble and making dangerous buildings safe.

WARTIME BATH: LIFE ON THE HOME FRONT 1939-45

On the third night of the Blitz, three high-explosive bombs were dropped on Westmoreland Street and Cheltenham Street, destroying dozens of homes and claiming the lives of Senior Warden Charles Bartlett and Warden Muriel Coates – the city's only female warden to die in the line of duty. This view shows the Sydenham Buildings/Westmoreland Street/Cheltenham Street neighbourhood shortly after the war once the debris of bomb-damaged buildings had been cleared. The water tower in the photograph of Cheltenham Street on page 98 is evident in this view at upper centre.

 The gutted ruins of St James's church (south side), set alight and burnt by incendiary bombs in the early hours of Monday 27 April. Note the emergency water tank beside the church wall for use by the fire service.

Damage to Nos 4 and 5 Lansdown Place East. Dr Sammy Marle was returning home at the height of the first raid and later wrote: 'The roads were already crackling with glass as we went up the hill ... a Hun plane above flew over machine-gunning & cannon-firing wildly round about ... then crash went a bomb just in front of Lansdown Place East.' (*Pat Woods*)

the Francis Hotel in Queen Square were 'sliced in halves'. At the Regina there was terrible loss of life. On the other side of the city he found:

'Oldfield Road, Lower Oldfield Road and most of East Twerton a shambles – quite a gay party: I've never seen the medical men of Bath looking so tired and worn, poor devils. I must have looked just the same, I suppose – they all did their job most stoutly and the only thing that failed was the telephone and the Warden system. Too many of the sub-wardens stayed in their homes apparently (so I've heard) so that the Home Guard had to get busy in their place.

'The number of miraculous escapes was legion, as you may imagine. Dr MacQuiston and his family under the dining room table had a direct hit, which demolished the house [at 110 Lower Oldfield Park], but they were all alive and unharmed. So also old Professor Edgeworth from Bristol. So odd, he and his sister crept out from the ruins of their houses [20 Combe Park, Weston] unhurt – direct hit and all – simply immortal!

'Mary Middlemass [Dr] and two of her sisters were not so fortunate for they were crushed. And the spirit of the people was superb – more determined than ever to put Hitler down. One of my section of the Home Guard had lost his house and furniture (he was married at Christmas) but, poking his head into the window of my car, he said, "Never mind doctor, 'e ain't going to beat us yet, is 'er?"

'Water and gas went (as usual), but very quickly supplies were coming on – emergency meal centres were fixed and the homeless were either billeted or sent to "rest centres". We took in the Leech-Wilkinsons [Arthur Leech-Wilkinson, obstetrician and gynaecologist, 16 Camden Crescent] and a friend the first night, the Cuppages and Timmy and another child the next. So what with ourselves, the Andrewses, and additions we were a jolly communal party. Now Dr and Mrs Cuppage have arranged to get sufficient repair to go back and are sleeping in their cellar. Burke's [Dr Cuppage's] consulting room is functioning again and they are on the high road to recovery.'

Fragments of stained glass from St Andrew's church, retrieved by Jack Falconer shortly after its destruction by incendiary bombs.

Devastation at the Regina Hotel on Bennett Street, where 27 guests lost their lives in the third attack during the early hours of Monday morning, 27 April.

On the Monday morning, Aubrey Jackman was staying with his mother at the Lansdown Grove Hotel and observed a 'little man' walking towards the front door:

> 'He was the same Ministry of Works official who had requisitioned the Pulteney Hotel. He now came to requisition the Lansdown Grove as an American Forces leave hostel. This was a blessing in disguise – the windows were blown out, ceilings fallen in and doors blown off. I slept under a table on what would have been the third night of the Blitz, but the Germans did not return.'

Naturally enough, the general feeling in the city was that the bombers would return again on the Monday night and many families who had not left on the Sunday decided to move out. Among the most popular places to take refuge were Sally-in-the-Woods at Bathford and the caves at Hampton Rocks. John Coe remembers watching crowds of people during the week following the Blitz:

> '... tramping up Widcombe Hill at dusk to take shelter in the caves at Hampton Rocks, fearful of further air-raids on the city. We were

without gas for many days, and our household had to make do with one electric ring for all food and water heating purposes. We were grateful for a free issue of American chocolate in the city.'

Joan Hurford and her family chose to take refuge in the caves at Hampton Rocks:

'Dad packed a small case. Carrying blankets we made our way to Hampton Rocks. There were many other families leaving the city for the same destination. At Hampton Rocks we didn't sleep much because it was cold. But we found it fascinating to watch the searchlights probing the sky. In the early hours the people who had been taking shelter with us began snaking their way back to the city. We did this for two nights, but thereafter we and our next-door neighbours went down into our cellar. At times it was really scary as we heard the drone of the planes overhead, not knowing whether they were "ours", and waiting for bombs to drop. I remember Dad saying, "If you hear the whine of the bomb falling, it won't be for you". After the bombing, I went back to school to find that a schoolmate in our class, Bernice Young, had been killed with all her family. Their house had received a direct hit. In grieving the loss of a friend, the full horror of war was brought home to us.'

Three men died in the third and final raid of the Blitz when the east wing of the Francis Hotel in Queen Square was devastated by a direct hit from a 500kg bomb.

Queen Square: the same view today showing the rebuilt Francis Hotel.

Thirteen-year-old Bernice, her three-rear-old baby sister Valerie and their mother Bertha died at their home, 17 Melrose Grove, off Southdown Road, in the second attack.

On the Monday night, Bob White's father was on Home Guard duty and didn't like the idea of his wife and teenage son being on their own at home should the raiders strike again.

'So my mother got a lift in a car and I got a lift on the back of a motorbike and we went out to Hinton Charterhouse where we stayed in a barn. That was the Monday night. Nothing happened that night or the night after that. The next night [Wednesday] we went down to an old barn at Combe Hay, all four of us in the car, and there was thousands of people coming down to Combe Hay! A lot of my pals were there. It was an uproarious night because they had brought bottles of beer with them. We were messing around chasing the girls. After that we went back to normal because we decided they [the bombers] weren't coming anymore.'

Some people in the Combe Down area took refuge in the stone quarries, where Pam Simmonds remembers feeling 'really safe from the bombing'.

Eileen Rogers worked for the Admiralty at Foxhill. Although she had had little sleep on the Sunday night, on the next morning she had to get up as usual and get ready to go to work. Needless to say, there were no buses. She recalled:

'Everything was at a standstill, so I walked up behind Entry Hill where there was a little lane that went into Foxhill, but there was a field to cross. And when I got to the field with a friend, there was a crater with all this clay all piled up and you had to scramble across to get to the office. In the meantime, my mother and father had been in touch with a friend at Timsbury who said for us to go out there for the rest of the week. The buses were very few and far between, so the problem was how to get to Timsbury. My mother and younger sister managed to get there, but I had to wait on the corner at the top of Wellsway with other people who lived out at Timsbury to get a lift. Well, a lorry came by with two huge tree trunks trailing behind, so we got on there, sitting astride these tree trunks, and off out to Timsbury!

We stayed for the rest of the week, but of course the sirens didn't go again, but I never felt safe again until peace was proclaimed.'

Pam Simmonds' mother had a cousin living at Box, and the family went there by train from Bath. 'We were directed to the schoolroom where sleeping accommodation had been provided on the floor for people coming from Bath. The next morning, we had breakfast with mum's cousin and caught the train back to Bath.'

Many of those made homeless were taken into people's houses in Bath and district until things could be sorted out. Dr and Mrs Matthews took a large number of people into their home at Newbridge Hill. In a heavily censored letter to her daughters in New Mexico, written early in May 1942, Mrs Matthews describes the accommodation arrangements and the traumatising effect the raids had on little children:

'Bath is beginning to settle down again, and all the thousands of homeless people are gradually being [censored] ... on Friday we visited the house at Kelston where we have had as many as 87 people sleeping on the floor some nights, and [censored] ... found homes for them. I think it would make your heart ache if you could see what a mess the two nights' raids have made of our beloved Bath...

'We all more or less live in my bedroom because we have got people sleeping in all the other rooms except the sitting room, which is rather a mess as all the windows were blown right out and there are holes in the ceiling. I haven't had the energy or time to clear it up yet. Our little boy Brian [one of the homeless children] is getting on wonderfully well. His little three-year-old brother was killed, and his mother is in hospital, but she is getting better. He told us that he had saved £1 in his money box to buy a bomber, which was in the Corridor toy-shop [Commons], but he didn't think he wanted a bomber now and he would rather have a very little aeroplane. Poor little chap. I should think he has had enough of bombers for the rest of his life. Sue [their youngest daughter] was very, very, good, but the noise frightened her, and she says every night, "I hope Hitler won't bomb us tonight, Mummy". And I have to stay somewhere near her until she is asleep. Brian is very good too, until he is put to bed, and then he screams for someone to stay with him.'

Valerie Ford and her family were made homeless when a 1,000kg high explosive bomb was dropped behind their terraced house at 15 Coronation Avenue. She remembers how her family and neighbours, whose homes had also been devastated, were taken to the Moravian Church Hall in Coronation Avenue:

'There we were given hot soup and a piece of two-inch-thick bread, which was most welcome. On hearing that we were homeless, relatives came to fetch us and we all went to live with my grandmother in her cottage at Fosse Lane, Batheaston. We lived there for the next two and a half years while our house was rebuilt, and went to the village school. My parents made frequent trips to our bombed house in Bath to salvage what they could. All our furniture, etc., was stored in lock-up garages at Batheaston. I well remember going with my mother once a week to polish the furniture, which my father, a carpenter by trade, had made himself.

'The front of our house in Coronation Avenue was still standing, along with its front door made by my father, in which he took a great pride because it was grained (the fashion at that time). One day he arrived at the house to find that the front door had been removed. With his screwdriver, he went in search of the door, and eventually found it hung on a house at the top of the avenue. He knocked and asked for the return of the door, which he carried back to our house. The same door is still on the house today, but painted white.'

Dr Ted Matthews' youngest daughter, Sue, with 'Brian the Blitzed', his arm in a sling. Brian was taken in by the Matthews family after he was bombed out of his home. His mother was badly injured and his three-year-old brother was killed in the raids. Sadly, Brian died of TB a year later. (*Bridget Wakefield*)

Just after the war started, Betty Cottle, her sister and their parents had moved from an old house in Holloway to a house on the newly-built estate at Whiteway Circle. They had an indoor shelter, a Morrison, which had a 'mesh cage all the way round'. Her father put a big mattress in the shelter and when the siren went 'he used to put us youngsters in there, and then when it was all over we used to go back to bed. It was a beautiful shelter because my sister and I always used to get up there on it and tap dance!'

'But of course, when it did begin to get really bad in Bath with the Blitz, that's when we all started going down to the fields to sleep at Warwick's Farm – that's near to where the cemetery is, at Haycombe. We'd either go down the cemetery lane and along by Ware's nurseries as it was, and go along a little path, or we'd go from Haycombe Drive into Pennyquick, and then we'd go

down the side of this field and along this track again. The farmer used to let our mum and our family and Mrs Bidwell and Mrs Dale across the road sleep there. She had a big family, and we used to go down there and he used to allow us to sleep in this barn.'

It was on the Monday evening when Pamela Taylor and her parents were recovering at St Martin's from their ordeal, that her mother's cousin and her uncle and aunt who lived at Priston came to fetch them after hearing about what had happened. With them also went Pamela's grandparents. They stayed on the family farm at Priston for the next three or four weeks. However, Percy and Elsie Taylor returned to bomb-ravaged Bath the next day to see what could be salvaged from the ruins of their home in Milton Avenue. To their horror, they found that the house had been looted. However, Mrs Kingston, a kindly neighbour, had managed to remove a number of their precious belongings for safekeeping. Pamela's prize possession was her piano:

 The view today looking towards Lymore Terrace and Valerie Ford's home beyond in Coronation Avenue, with South Twerton School (now renamed Oldfield Park Junior School) on the left. The six houses in Lymore Terrace and several in the lower part of Coronation Avenue were later rebuilt after suffering extensive blast and fire damage from the 1,000kg 'Hermann' high-explosive bomb that fell in the allotments behind them.

'It was by the chimney breast with my dolls stuck on top. I loved my dolls and although I was only 14, mum had done them up so that when I was married, I could give them to my children. Dad's car was squashed because we had taken the force of the blast that had come between the two houses, but we had taken more of it on our side. We had a budgerigar called Jimmy who could not be found. Dad went to the hole we got out of and he called, and there was a whistle and the budgie came out. Dad put him in his pocket and went down Holloway where he got a cage in an old shop for half a crown. The bird lived for a number of years. Now I expect what had happened was the bird was on a table in the dining room and he must have come down with the table and flown out of his cage.'

Henderson, one of the Falconers' billetees, had his wife and daughter Pat staying with him during the Blitz weekend. A New Forest surveyor seconded to the Admiralty for the duration, he worked at an office in Portland Place. On the Monday morning, Ivor Barnsdale, the Falconers' other billetee, returned to Brunswick Place and arrived at the same time as Henderson, who had come from fire-watching duty in Portland Place. They found the house empty – the Falconers had hired a car from Mr Frederick Bannister's garage at 6 Belvedere to take them to Swainswick, where they stayed with friends for a week or two. In the meantime, Ivor slept at his office every night for a week, and the following weekend gratefully 'accepted an offer from a colleague to sleep "between the sheets".' He went to bed at 3pm and awoke 24 hours later!

Some of those families who had lost their homes in the raids were evacuated to various villages outside the city. Some went to Box, while others were put up in what were then the Parish Rooms (later the village shop) in Bathampton. Some were also put up in the church, but Brian Hamilton remembers that they didn't stay long. 'They had all gone from the church in the middle of the night as they considered it too eerie!'

A fine example to people living in Britain's blitz-torn cities was set by the King and Queen. They were at Buckingham Palace when it was struck by a bomb during the Battle of Britain. The royal couple later visited many bombed towns and cities across the nation and are seen here during their 90-minute visit to Bath on Saturday 2 May 1942.

WARTIME BATH: LIFE ON THE HOME FRONT 1939-45

The village of Freshford lies in the Avon valley on the Somerset/Wiltshire border, some 6 miles south-east of Bath. It, too, did its bit to succour those who had been bombed out of their homes in the city. Fay Inchfawn (real name Elizabeth Rebecca Ward) was one of Britain's most prolific women authors of the interwar years. *Salute to the Village*, first published in 1943, was her first-hand account of the impact of the Second World War on Freshford, and it describes how the village rose to the occasion after the Blitz on Bath:

'That Sunday night the raiders came again, and again John and I got up. This second attack was worse than the first. The glow in the sky opposite our front door was blood red, like the Northern Lights. Within myself I was truly and thoroughly frightened. That fear-striking drone of heavy planes overhead – all those thunderous bangs and explosions – would they never cease?

'The Village had naturally been up all night and on Monday morning, in the absence of instruction but in the presence of such dire necessity, it was decided to open up the Rest Centre, which had been carefully arranged and equipped ready for the catastrophe of invasion.

'The National School was appointed the place, and Mrs Firth and Mrs Ellison were the ladies in charge. That Monday morning the scholars were gleefully dispersed, and the schoolrooms were cleared for action. A band of helpers assembled. Oil stoves from a consignment sent by the USA to every hospital in Britain were commandeered. Mr Hazeldean supplied breads, cooked meats, margarine, buns and cakes. Piles of sandwiches were cut. Milk, mattresses, easy chairs, blankets, rugs were delivered in procession.

'A board with the word "REST" upon it was set up in the school yard, and in the afternoon the victims of the raid began to come in. Two elderly women were the first to arrive. They had walked the whole way – five miles – and were dead beat. They stood at the School House door asking whether they might come in, and could they be given shelter for the night?

'After that there was a rush. By train, bus, on lorries and in vans, refugees came to our Rest Centre. They all carried bundles or baggage of some kind, and all made the same inquiry: might they stay all night? Anywhere just to feel safe – on the floor, in a chair, just a roof over them and to be free from fear. ... The forty-eight hours which is the usual limit for keeping Rest Centres open was extended to a week.'

BLITZ – THE AFTERMATH

Raymond Jones, a Bath schoolmaster at West Central School and acting organist of the Abbey for the duration of the war, was living with his parents in Elm Place on Bear Flat. They escaped lightly with only one window shattered and a few doors blown off their hinges. When the 'all-clear' sounded, Raymond made his way to Beechen Cliff, climbing over piles of rubble, glass and tiles – all that was left of the bank and other buildings on Bear Flat. From Beechen Cliff 'it looked as though the whole city was in flames':

This dramatic view of the Abbey seen through bombed houses in Wellsway was taken by Noel Harbutt shortly after the Blitz. Many (especially Bristol-based Aardman Animations, creators of *Wallace & Gromit*) will remember the Harbutt family for the modelling material called Plasticine, invented by William Harbutt in 1897 and made in their factory at Bathampton.

'Early the next morning I made my way to the Abbey. There were scenes of destruction on all sides, and a heavy pall of smoke hanging everywhere. Although the Abbey itself did not sustain a direct hit, the damage by blast from a bomb that fell nearby was enormous. Inside the Abbey I met the Archdeacon [the Venerable William Marshall Selwyn, who was also Rector] and a small group of Abbey officials; everyone was in a state of complete shock. The east window was gone, and it was a pathetic sight to see great gaps in the clerestory with shattered glass hanging precariously by the leadwork.

'The organ was of course my main concern, but it was impossible to get up the stairs into the loft because of shattered glass and leadwork. The organ fills the whole of the north transept, and many thousands of pipes are very close to the windows. With much of the glass blown out, the organ was completely exposed to wind and rain. I knew that this would cause untold damage unless some form of protection could be quickly forthcoming. Fortunately, I was able to convince the Archdeacon that this should be given absolute priority, and in a matter of days workmen were able to hang enormous tarpaulins over the inside of the transept walls. When this was done, I remember the Archdeacon saying to me with a wry smile, "I hope you are happier now about your precious organ!"

'It took me many hours of work removing the debris from the organ loft stairs and from the loft itself. But apart from pulling shattered glass and broken leadwork from the mouths of the very large pedal pipes, there was very little else I could do – the cleaning of the organ had to be left to experts. I made sure that it was impossible to switch on the blowing apparatus until all risk of damage to the leatherwork of the wind reservoirs was removed. But at least the organ was dry!'

The final comments made be Dr Sammy Marle in a letter to his children probably reflect the feelings of many people in Bath after the events of that terrible weekend. Early in May 1942 he wrote:

'So there you are – a most dastardly attack on a defenceless population. We've got Hitler rattled, I do believe, or he wouldn't do such silly ass things. If he imagines he can break us that way he has far less intelligence than I give him credit for. He is an ass – a dirty one – and his foul air force no more than murderers. No one minds a hoot about Stothert's, or the Gas Works, or the Station: that's all right, let him do as he likes with them. But to fly up and down above the roofs shooting off his guns and cannons into the dwelling houses of the poor is such a foul crime that no one will forgive him such villainy. And how we can still be expected (if one is brought down and any of the crew remain alive) to save them, I cannot see. They ask for death and should have it served out to them. Well, well, I've always been a man of peace, but it hardly seems so now.'

One of the few happy outcomes of the Blitz happened to Phyllis Bond. When she married early in the war, her husband had left his dog, named Paddy, with his mother. In the first night of the raids the dog disappeared.

'We all thought he must have been killed. No animals were allowed into the street shelters. But one morning, several weeks after the Blitz, I was in the Post Office when the door was pushed open and in flew Paddy. He'd sniffed me out! It seemed that during the raid he'd run all the way to Radstock where a man took him in and looked after him. The man worked out that he must have come from the Twerton side of Bath and if he let him off the lead he'd nose out somebody belonging to him, and this is what he did.'

A sad epilogue to the Blitz appeared in the *Bath Weekly Chronicle* on 23 May 1942:

'Somewhere in Bath Central Police Station is a grim card index of human suffering – a collection of photographs. They are not pleasant photographs. But one day they may be the means of wiping from someone's mind the saddest burden that anyone can bear – uncertainty. For these are photographs of those victims of the raids on Bath who have not been – or cannot be – identified. Ever since the Blitz the police have been taking these photographs in the hope that they will eventually help trace the identity of those who died unknown.'

This distressing photographic record is still in existence, but for obvious reasons it is not available for inspection by the general public.

Many years later, the Reverend John Coe found himself involved in a small footnote to the Blitz:

'Pat, aged five in 1942, had moved from London to Bath with her parents, her father's work being with the Admiralty. They rented a house in King Edward Road [No 11], and on the fateful weekend were entertaining his brother and wife seeking some peace from the raids on Plymouth. When the bombs started falling [on 25/26 April], the two ladies and the child crammed themselves into the Anderson shelter in the garden, but there was no room for the two men. The house received a direct hit and both the men were killed. The occupants of the Anderson shelter were dug out by rescue workers hours later. The mother and child eventually returned to London by train in borrowed clothes. On 6 October 1997, Pat, who had not visited Bath since the war, brought the ashes of her mother, Mary Miller, to be buried by me in the communal grave at Haycombe Cemetery, where her father's name [Alfred Walter Miller] is on one of the many monumental stones. A poignant moment of remembrance for us of a childhood's tragedy.'

BLITZ – THE AFTERMATH

An aerial photograph of the upper part of the Georgian city taken in 1953, eight years after the end of the war, tells its own tale. The bomb-damaged houses in the Royal Crescent, the Circus, Circus Mews (Norton Dairies), and Julian Road, have been rebuilt, but the Assembly Rooms, restored shortly before the war at great expense and gutted in the Blitz, remain in a ruined state as do Margaret Chapel and houses in Margaret's Buildings. St Andrew's church is a burned-out shell and its spire has been taken down. The monstrosities that replaced the artisans' dwellings in Morford Street and Ballance Street have yet to be built, but the 'Sack of Bath' was already underway as redevelopment of Northampton Street and Harley Street shows. The wartime 'Dig for Victory' allotments in front of the Royal Crescent are still being cultivated.

CHAPTER 6
BOMBER'S RETURN

When 87-year-old Willi Schludecker visited Bath on 25 April 2008, it was as an invited guest of the city. Exactly 66 years before, he was piloting a German Dornier Do 217 bomber that had unloaded some 4,000kg of bombs onto the streets of Bath during a night of terror for its unprepared inhabitants.

At the invitation of Bath resident Chris Kilminster, who had lost family in the Blitz including his grandparents, Willi returned to the city he helped partly destroy to make a public apology. Talking about the Bath raids, he said: 'It is a thing to remember and think about. It was a sad and bitter time. I am here as we came in 1942 and we did a lot of damage. We didn't realise it at the time. I come again to say sorry. Thanks for the welcome. I never expected such a reception.'

In 1942, Feldwebel (Sergeant) Willi Schludecker was a pilot with Kampfgeschwader 2 (KG2), a Luftwaffe bomber squadron stationed in Holland. He had never heard of Bath before the pre-mission briefing in the late afternoon of 25 April. KG2 was usually based at Gilze-Rijen, but it was brought south to Evreux in Normandy for the Baedeker raids on south-west England. Remembering his family loss, Chris said that it was an emotional decision to invite Willi to Bath. 'They were killed when a bomb hit an air-raid shelter, I find it difficult to talk about. It still chokes me up. But there are no hard feelings against Willi. He was just doing his job and was never a supporter of the Nazi party.'

Wearing his wartime Luftwaffe uniform and medals, Willi was guest of honour at a civic reception in the Guildhall where he was

German bomber pilot Willi Schludecker revisited Bath as an invited guest of the city on 25 April 2008. He was presented with a copy of *Bath at War: The Home Front* by co-author Jonathan Falconer.

Dressed in his wartime Luftwaffe uniform, Willi was greeted in the Guildhall at a formal reception in the Mayor's Parlour.

welcomed by the Mayor. He spoke no English, but his words of apology to the people of Bath were translated into English and delivered by his friend Richard Flohr-Swann, who accompanied him on their visit to the city.

Willi's memories of the raids were translated from German by Richard Flohr-Swann and feature on the website of the Bath Blitz Memorial Project. Extracts are reproduced here with the Project's kind permission:

'Between April and July 1942, when I was 22 years old, I took part in attacks on England, from bases in Holland and France. In April 1942, I took part in the first two raids on your city during the Bath Blitz. On the occasion of the third attack, I had to return to base before reaching the target, due to failure of the left engine.

'There were rumours that Churchill himself and high-ranking planners from the Navy were in Bath. It was not just the Dornier Do 217 bombers from Kampfgeschwader 2 that were ordered to attack, but also at least two other squadrons with Junkers Ju 88 and Heinkel He 111 were involved in the raids. My target was the city centre. I was not informed how Bath was protected.

'When I joined the Air Force I was very young and I just wanted to fly. I did not think much about the future. But when I started flying operational missions, I soon realised the dangers of my job and then I lived only from flight to flight. You must understand that the average survival time for a bomber pilot flying over Great Britain was only seven missions.

'I still have a copy of my flight log. It shows that on the 23rd and 24th April 1942, I took part in the raids on Exeter. On the 25th it shows: "Take-off from Evreux at 2208 for Bath. Attack height 1200m [3,937ft] in target area. Some flak and spotlighting. One twin-engined night-fighter going after me. Returned to base 26th at 0055."

'On 26th it shows: "Take-off from Evreux at 0343, head for Bath. Attack height 1600m [5,250ft]. Returned to base at 0642."

'On 27th it shows: "Take-off from Evreux at 0042, head for Bath. Engine failure (left engine) 2800m [9,190ft]. Bombs dropped near Portland. Returned to base at 0253."

'My engine was repaired during the 27th and according to my log I took off for a test flight at 1618, landing again at 1747, and then at 2333 I took off for a raid on Ipswich and Northampton.'

WARTIME BATH: LIFE ON THE HOME FRONT 1939-45

After the German invasion of Russia in June 1941, the transfer of resources to the Eastern Front had left only weak bomber forces in the West. The Luftwaffe had to cast around to pull together enough aircraft to comply with the Führer's order for retaliatory strikes on English cities after the RAF raids on Rostock and Lübeck. A transcript of a secret recording held in the UK National Archives of a conversation between two captured Luftwaffe aircrew who had been involved in the Baedeker raids, reveals how German aircrew were uncomfortable with the small numbers of aircraft that were involved:

Airman 1: The Führer made a speech on Sunday. What did he say?

Airman 2: I thought it was going to be something new. Well, he said nothing like that at all. Only that England would now be subjected without pause to reprisals by the German Air Force. They (the English) must also have heard that, and expected us to attack with thousands of aircraft. I was horrified when I heard how few aircraft we could muster.

Luftflotte 3, whose bomber units were based in occupied France, Belgium and Holland, planned the raids on Bath for the moonlight period at the end of April. They were to replicate tactics successfully used by the RAF against German towns and cities, where the attacking force was concentrated over the target in a raid of short duration in order to swamp the defences.

In the first raid, which took place late in the evening of 25 April, the main German bomber force comprised some 80 aircraft drawn from II and III/KG 2 (flying from Evreux and Amsterdam/Schipol respectively), and II/KG 40 (Soesterberg in northern Holland) equipped with Dornier Do 217s, as well as Kü Fl Gr 106, an anti-shipping unit equipped

Air and ground crews from Willi's unit, Kampfgeschwader 2 (KG2), relax on the grass at Evreux, their airfield in northern France, before take-off for a raid on England in spring 1942. In the background is a Dornier Do 217E of the type used over Bath. (*Bundesarchiv 1011-362-2212-39*)

As a 21-year-old Dornier Do 217 bomber pilot, Willi took part in the first two Baedeker raids on Bath on 25–26 April 1942. Willi died on 17 June 2010, at the age of 90, in Cologne with his daughter at his bedside. (*Willi Schludecker*)

with Junkers Ju 88s (Dinard, Brittany), while I/KG 2 (Gilze Rijen, Holland) with about 25 Do 217s joined the attack a little later.

On 25 April, the Luftwaffe flew a total of 151 bomber sorties to Bath, with most aircraft making two trips. Having returned to their bases after the initial raid, they were rearmed and refuelled and took off again at 03.30hrs, arriving over Bath at about 04.40hrs on the 26th. The second attack lasted for just over an hour. Crews claimed to have dropped 206 tonnes of high explosives and 3,564 incendiary bombs on the city in the biggest effort against Britain since July 1941. The Anzünders (fire-lighters) from Erprobungs und Lehrkommando 100 (Ergr u Lehr Kdo 100) were operating that night using the electronic navigation aid Y-Verfahren, successfully leading in the other participating units from II and III/KG 2, II/KG 40, Kü Fl Gr 106 and Kü Fl Gr 506, in addition to the various aircraft from the fourth Gruppen. Bath was the target again in the early hours of the following morning (Monday 27th) with all bomber units from Luftflotte 3 being utilised, including for the first time the fourth Gruppen with their pupil crews, of which IV/KG 2, IV/KG 3, IV/KG 4, IV/KG 30, IV/KG 55 and IV/KG 77 were on the battle order flying a mixed bag of obsolete Do 17s, He 111s and Ju 88s. Once the aircraft arrived over the city at

The Junkers Ju 88A-4 dive-bomber was another of the aircraft types that was used on the Bath raids. This aircraft is from Küstenfliegergruppe 106 (KüFlGr 106) based at Dinard in Brittany, one of two coastal patrol units that were drafted in to make up numbers. (*Bundesarchiv 1011-356-1805-24A*)

1.25am, they were able to fly around at will in a bright moonlit sky, making extensive use of shallow dive-bombing, and machine-gunning the streets. With and no anti-aircraft guns or balloon barrage, Bath was virtually unprotected against air attack. Willi Schludecker again:

'The Dornier 217 had a crew of four. We navigated our own zig-zag route to avoid night-fighters. During the flight, the gunner and the radio operator were ordered to lie on the floor, look down through the glass, and report any flash from the barrel of an ack-ack gun. If anything was spotted, I immediately changed the plane's direction. There was a short time between seeing the flash and the shot reaching our flying height, and this method gave us the best chance of avoiding the flak.'

Flying at low level to avoid being detected by English radar, the German bomber crews could see the glow on the horizon of Bath burning even before they crossed over the coast into Dorset. Willi decided not to follow the radio navigational beam directing them to their target some 60 miles ahead, knowing it would give away their position to RAF fighters lying in wait for them.

'I had no contact with the other bombers. During the flight we had to maintain radio silence, so all the aircraft were flying completely on their own, even though all had the same destination.

'The only time the radio was used was when each plane was over its target and had dropped its bombs. Then they had to make just one radio transmission, which was to say: "Dropping at time xx:xx", giving the exact time. With this one transmission on long-range short-wave radio it was possible, by cross-

checking the radio waves when the message was received, to verify that the plane had been over the target. I had not received any complaints for not having been over my targets, which confirmed that I had successfully navigated to Bath each time.

'Of course, at that time I was not aware of the awful damage our bombardment had caused. But only now, on my first visit to Bath, have I seen all of the pictures taken on the ground here after the attacks. I am deeply touched by what I have seen and I realise that the war caused dreadful harm to your city and its people.

'The only thing I can do now is to ask you all for forgiveness for any pain that I might have caused and any damage that I might have inflicted when I came to your city in 1942. Please accept my sincere apology.'

During the war, Willi flew more than 120 bombing and mine-laying sorties over England, Russia and the Balkans. He was shot down four times and crashed-landed 23 times. On 23/24 July 1942, he was on his way to bomb Bedford when his Dornier Do 217 was intercepted over the East Coast of England by an RAF Bristol Beaufighter from 409 (RCAF) Squadron flown by Flt Lt Peter McMillan. In the ensuing engagement the Dornier was badly damaged but Willi managed to coax it back across the North Sea to Holland where he crash-landed at Gilze-Rijen, suffering severe injuries when he put the aircraft down at three times its normal landing speed. As a result, he spent five months in hospital. In 1945 he returned to active service as the Allies closed in on Germany, flying a further 30 missions before his squadron was grounded owing to a shortage of fuel and ammunition.

After the war he declined an invitation to join the re-formed Luftwaffe, saying: 'They misused me once (*continued on page 125*)

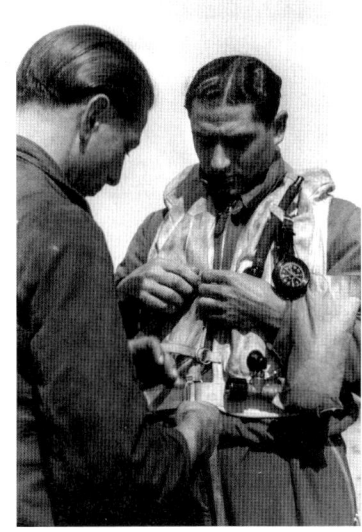

Oberleutnant Karl Rueck flew a post-raid photo-reconnaissance sortie over Bath on 29 April in a Messerschmitt Bf109 specially adapted for the task. On 17 December, Rueck and his wingman Leutnant Karl Raucheisen were on another reconnaissance mission when they were shot down into the English Channel by RAF fighters and lost without trace.

GERMAN BOMBER UNITS OPERATING AGAINST BATH ON 25-27 APRIL 1942

Unit	Base	Aircraft type
I/KG2	Gilze Rijen, NL	Do 217E/K
II/KG2	Evreux, France from Soesterberg	Do 217E
III/KG2	Amsterdam-Schipol, NL	Do 217E
IV/KG2	possibly Juvincourt, France	Do 17Z and 217
II/KG40	Soesterberg, NL	Do 217
Kü Fl Gr 106	Dinard, France	Ju 88A
Kü Fl Gr 506	Leeuwarden, NL	Ju 88A
Ergr.u.Lehr Kdo 100	Chartres, France	He 111H
IV/KG3	Brussels-Evere, Belgium	Do 17, Ju 88A
IV/KG4	Avord, France	He 111H

First attack, 25 April c.23.20–00.10 – c.80 bombers
Second attack, 26 April c.04.40–05.30 – c.80 bombers
Third (and final) attack, 27 April c.01.25–02.05 – 83 bombers.

The German raiders did not have it all their own way: some bombers were shot down by RAF fighters, while others were damaged in combat and only just made it back across the Channel to their bases.

During the same period, RAF Bomber Command raided Rostock on four consecutive nights between 23/24 and 26/27 April, during which eight bombers were lost. Below is a list of German losses from the Blitz weekend.

25 April
22.30
Ju 88 of Küstenfliegergruppe 506 (Kü Fl Gr 506) shot down by 307 Sqn Beaufighter from Exeter, 15 miles S of Beer Head, Devon.
23.50
Ju 88A-6 of IV./Kampfgeschwader 3 (KG 3) shot down by 255 Sqn Beaufighter from High Ercall, near Builth Wells, Brecon.

26 April
00.11
Do 17Z of IV./KG 2 shot down by 219 Sqn Beaufighter from Tangmere, crashed into sea off French coast near Courseulles sur Mer, Normandy.

05.00
Do 217E-4 of II./KG 40 dazzled by searchlights, flew into Bottlebush Down, near Handley Cross, Dorset.

27 April
00.47
Ju 88 of IV./KG 30, damaged in combat with 307 Sqn Beaufighter from Exeter, returned to base in France.
01.05
Ju 88 of IV./KG 4 damaged in combat with 604 Sqn Beaufighter from Middle Wallop, made it back to Avord, Loire valley.

01.15
Ju 88 of Kü Fl Gr 506 damaged in combat with 307 Sqn Beaufighter from Exeter, 10 miles S of the city, made it back to emergency landing at Dinard-St Brieuc, Brittany.
01.40
Do 17Z of IV./KG 2, damaged in combat over Lansdown with 87 Sqn Hurricane from Charmy Down, crashed into sea on way home.
02.15
He 111 of IV./KG 55 damaged in combat near Bristol with 125 Sqn Defiant from Colerne, landed back at Rennes, Brittany.

One of a sequence of photographs taken over Bath by a Spitfire from the RAF's No 1 Photographic Reconnaissance Unit on 27 April 1942. At the top centre of the photograph is Alexandra Park and the streets of 'Poet's Corner' at Bear Flat to its right. The river Avon can be seen meandering its way across the picture from centre left to centre bottom, with Bath Spa station at centre left and the LMS station at Green Park centre bottom.

This general view of the city was taken by the Luftwaffe's Oberleutnant Karl Rueck from 1.(F)/123 on 29 April. Alexandra Park is just below centre right while the Avon flows from centre right to top left. The Admiralty site at Foxhill is at bottom right, with the Circus and Royal Crescent at top right. The image has been annotated by photographic interpreters to identify areas of bomb damage and cratering.

before and I didn't want to give them the chance to do it again.'

Bath was still reeling from the effects of two nights of bombing when a Spitfire reconnaissance aircraft from No 1 Photo Reconnaissance Unit took off from RAF Benson in Oxfordshire in the early afternoon of the 27th to photograph damage to the city. Normally, the unit's task was to photograph cities in occupied Europe to assess results after Bomber Command had visited them, only this time it was photographing an English city after the Luftwaffe had called. The high-level coverage from about 25,000ft shows veils of smoke obscuring neighbourhoods like Cheltenham Street and Westmoreland Street on the Lower Bristol Road, while north of the river St Andrew's church and buildings on Julian Road are still smouldering.

An aerial view of Bath appeared on the front page of the 19 June edition of *Luftflotte West*. This was a weekly 'propaganda' magazine for Luftflotte 3, which was based in German-occupied areas of Northern France, the Netherlands, Belgium, and Vichy France. The cover flash at bottom right says 'Bath after the German retaliatory attack'.

Two days later, keen to confirm the damage inflicted on the city by its bombers, the Luftwaffe ordered its own high-level photo-reconnaissance mission to photograph Bath. A damage assessment sortie was planned for the 27th, but unfavourable weather had led to its cancellation. Conditions had improved by the 29th and a sortie was made by an experienced recce pilot named Karl Rueck of 1.(F)/123 – Aufklärungsgruppe (Reconnaissance Group) 123. Oberleutnant Rueck took off from Toussus-le-Buc airfield, 11 miles southwest of Paris, flying a Messerschmitt Bf109-F4/R3 that had been specially adapted from the fighter version of the Bf109 for aerial reconnaissance work. Weather conditions over Bath were good and Rueck took a sequence of clear photographs that revealed the damage and destruction. One of these photographs subsequently appeared a couple of months later on the front cover of *Luftflotte West*, the official magazine of the Luftwaffe's Luftflotte 3.

CHAPTER 7
FOOD, FUN AND CHEWING GUM

For those who experienced life on the Home Front at first hand, the years 1939 to 1945 mean different things to different people. Some remember it for the blackout, others for the food shortages, while a few individuals still remember the war for the 'regulation' five inches of bath water they were allowed! For many, their strongest memories of daily life in wartime are focused on how they obtained their food, what they did in their spare time and – love them or loathe them – the Yanks.

Food rationing was introduced in stages. Local food offices had been set up across Britain on the outbreak of war and, before long, National Registration took place. This provided a list of everybody in the country and their addresses, and in due course the Food Office began to prepare food ration books based on this information. The central Food Office in Bath was located at the Octagon in Milsom Street. Phyllis Bond was laid-up in bed suffering with shingles at her home in Albany Road, Twerton, when the news of food rationing came through:

'Everybody had to register with a particular shop, the choice was yours, and it was a well-known fact in those days that if you put a printed form in front of the average Englishman he couldn't fill it up. So, as I was home in bed at the time, I offered to do it for my husband's employer. I must have done hundreds because everybody had to register and because somebody else was doing it for them, they just rolled up.'

From 8 January 1940, bacon, ham, butter, and sugar were rationed. On 11 March meat rationing began on the financial basis of 1s 10d per week, with a half-ration for those under six, and this was followed on 8 July by tea, cooking fats, jam and cheese. When rationing of that staple of the English diet, tea, was introduced, it was described as a temporary measure! A different system was introduced for eggs and milk that were supplied to shops in proportion to the number of customers who had registered with them. Generally

Food ration books were issued to everyone and everyone had to register with a particular shop for the various provisions. This ration book (below left) belonged to John (Jack) Falconer, father and grandfather of the authors. Ration books were divided into sections that contained coupons for different commodities (below, belonging to David Falconer). These were redeemable against purchases and ensured that everyone had their fair share, no matter how meagre the quantity set by the government.

126

'The one o'clock whistle.' Munitions workers on foot and bicycles are seen hurrying along Victoria Bridge Road after leaving the Victoria Works of Stothert & Pitt Ltd. The firm made an important contribution to the war effort with weapons and equipment. The arduous physical work meant that workers in heavy industry were entitled to more food rations than the average citizen.

speaking, from then on the consumer was largely confined not only to those quantities, but also to the retailers with whom he or she had registered. Much later in the war, in June 1944, Joan Matthews, wife of the Newbridge GP, made a list of 'some of our present rations'. When one compares these quantities with what people expect to buy and consume in the 2020s, as well as the absence of so-called convenience foods, the contrast is staggering:

'Milk: 2½ pints a week. Margarine: 4oz. a week. Butter: 2oz. a week. Sugar: ½lb. a week. Meat ½lb. worth a week (enough for about two days). Fish: not rationed, but you can't often get it. Jam: 1lb. a month (sometimes there is an extra ration). Cheese: 3oz. a week. Bacon: 4oz. a week. Eggs: vary from 1 a week to 1 a month. We get 24 points a month and you have to give points for most things: porridge, breakfast cereals, rice, lentils, biscuits, tinned milk, fish or meat, syrup, etc. We hardly ever see any fresh or tinned fruit and we certainly don't get chicken or turkey for dinner. No ice cream is allowed to be made, and no fancy cakes, and the sweet ration is 3oz. a week.'

Eileen Wiggins remembers a 'dear old lady who lived in a cottage in Rossiter Road' coming into the Co-op in Widcombe Parade one morning:

'Her husband and one of her sons were firemen on the railway. But agricultural workers had to take sandwiches ... they had a 12oz cheese ration. There'd be special paper in the inside of their ration books. And this old dear used to come in. And other people came in, and there was one very irate lady who used to say "Who's going to 'ave that great lump of cheese?' And the times I showed the ration book ... and I said, "It's because he's a fireman".

'You see, there was no ham ... I mean, Spam didn't come in until the Americans came in. And the Spam was off the ration, and they were allowed perhaps two or three slices. But, I mean, cheese was all that you could have – you know. Well then, she used to come in on a Thursday for "our Ron's ration" – you know, but she was a dear old soul.

'And then the eggs. If you were an expectant mother you had a green ration book, and you had three eggs. Well, very often when the branch order came in, everything came in bar the eggs! And they'd come in... "Ain't them eggs in yet?" And I'd say, "No, we 'ant got them". "Well, 'ave I got to come back again?" I'd say, "I'm sorry".

'Sometimes they used to get really rude to us. I think they thought we were keeping them outside just for a lark, you know! And, "why is she 'aving three eggs?" Well [sigh], dear, oh dear! I'd say, "Well, expectant mothers and babies 'ave three on a book".

'We had some really awful people, you know. And then things like blancmange powder, custard powder, and jellies. We perhaps got two boxes. And I had this orange card with it marked down, and you had the date on top, and you marked it off. And you got people – it was always indelible pencil – but you got people that tried to rub it out and come round again, but we got to know them! And then of course we got the odd two-dozen currant buns, or two-dozen doughnuts, and they'd really fight over those when they're queuing up outside, you know. But, some of them were so greedy, it was the same people there every day, and I used to think to myself well, nobody else had a chance. You couldn't put them away for people, it was just "first come, first served".'

David Falconer remembers that his family was registered with John R. Huntley & Sons, the provision merchants at the bottom of Milsom Street, on the corner of Quiet Street. The assistant who usually dealt with our

FOOD, FUN AND CHEWING GUM

A clear plate means A clear conscience

Don't take more than you can eat

Wartime Britain was no place for 'eyes that were bigger than stomachs'. Food was rationed and many commodities had to be brought into the country by convoys of merchant ships at great cost in human lives and vessels lost to enemy U-boats.

order at the counter was a Mr Parsons who lived in Marlborough Buildings. Ration books were handed over the counter and, as the order was being put up, Mr Parsons marked off the coupons with a blue pencil. Frequently, a 'little extra' in the way of eggs, margarine, and bacon found its way into mother's shopping basket, with a nod and a wink from Mr Parsons. Mr Parsons was often invited to tea on Sunday afternoons!

On the south side of Princes Buildings was Broadhurst's, the fishmongers. Women (and sometimes men) queued first thing in the morning along the pavement outside Broadhurst's towards the top of Milsom Street. Sometimes the queue extended into Milsom Street itself. It seemed to some people that the owner (or manager) of the fishmonger's used to delight in keeping the queue of people waiting before he pulled up the shutters of the shop – especially on bitterly cold winter mornings. Once inside the shop, it was not uncommon to hear the telephone ring. Residents in the Circus and the Royal Crescent would not deign to join a queue for fish. Instead, they rang in with their orders and arranged delivery. One can just imagine how this was viewed by those who had queued for so long in the cold to get their meagre ration of fish.

Writing on 16 April 1942 to her daughter Judy in America, Joan Matthews was clearly feeling the strain and frustration of daily life in wartime Bath. Little did she know that the Baedeker Blitz was only ten days away:

> 'Life is such a terrible rush and things are pretty difficult. Instead of just ringing up Jefferies and ordering meat (and telling him what I think of him if it isn't nice), I have to trail down the road every morning and stand in a fish or a meat queue and be jolly thankful if I get anything at all. You have to queue for pretty nearly everything because there are not enough buses and not enough people to serve in the shops. It's such a waste of time...'

'Tim' Cuppage remembers the sacrifices her mother made to make sure she and her father had enough:

'She saved eggs (stored in a big earthenware jar, in isinglass) and fat for my birthday cake, etc., and she ate thin slices of bread and dripping, which was not healthy and probably contributed to her future heart problems. We ate pretty well, the local shopkeeper being very good to "the doctor". The fish and chip shop was a godsend.'

As far as Eileen Rogers was concerned, everything was in 'short supply':

'Butter was one of the things we missed most of all. You were given basic cooking margarine, which was horrible to spread on bread, so what most people did was to mix our butter and marg together to make it more palatable. In the summer when home-grown fruit like plums and apples were about, we were given an extra ration of sugar for jam-making. I remember one Christmas, I think it was 1942, things seemed to be very scarce somehow, and we had a Christmas cake, a "bought" one, but I think if there were two sultanas in it, I was exaggerating! The marzipan was as thin as a razor blade, and the icing too! It was all very plain and horrible, but it was a Christmas cake, and you did keep up the tradition because it was Christmas. Germans or no Germans, we were going to have our Christmas pudding and a cake. You put things like grated carrot in your Christmas pudding.

 The old Co-operative Society shop in Coronation Avenue where Valerie Ford's father did his fire-watching duty is still there today, but has long since closed its doors. During the war years (and later) such shops were the mainstay of local communities in the city before their gradual demise as a result of supermarkets cornering the food market. Eileen Rogers' mother liked to shop there so she could get her 'divvy'.

'Sweets were rationed, but our mother and father used to let us have their sweet ration. Meat was in very short supply. We used to eat rabbit, which made a good meal. It was a question of trying to eke things out. We got our provisions from the Co-op grocery in Coronation Avenue – we used to get all our stuff there. There was a little shop across the road, but we used to deal with the Co-op because Mum liked the "divvy" [dividend stamps].'

With the outbreak of war, citrus fruits like oranges and lemons had become virtually unobtainable almost overnight. When a rare consignment of oranges arrived in the city on 17 May 1942, the *Chronicle* thought it newsworthy enough to report that 'on Friday evening there was a queue outside a fruit shop for oranges'. However, in 1943, oranges became more plentiful in the shops and by the autumn they were made available to every ration book holder at the rate of 1lb per person.

The first general allocation of oranges was made in February 1944, although distribution was confined to areas within easy distance of the port of landing. In the case of Bath this was Avonmouth. In fact, oranges in plentiful quantity had arrived in the city during mid-February and were sold 'off-ration'. But the enjoyment was short-lived for retailer and customer alike, because so many had turned bad, having been so long in transit. Eileen Rogers remembers the occasion:

'This rumour went round that this ship had come in at Avonmouth with a consignment of oranges, so we all queued up. I think we had to go into Bath for them. I don't know how many we were allowed each, but there were five of us so we had quite a nice collection of oranges! And that afternoon and evening we did make pigs of ourselves – we were all bilious that night!'

In 1944, small supplies of lemons were distributed in some areas of England. Bath received its share in time for Shrove Tuesday, 22 February, for citizens to squeeze on their pancakes. The allocation to Bath's wholesalers and retailers was on the same basis as for oranges, but supplies were insufficient to allow as much as a pound per person. Even so, much of what had been commonplace before the war remained unobtainable to most people, as Eileen recalls:

'No tinned fruit, no bananas. My father had some friends who used to go out shooting, and I remember he came home with some pigeons. Mum stuffed them – they weren't very big, but that made a meal. Dad did know somebody in Spear's, I think it was the manager, and he used to sometimes come home with an extra bit of bacon, or some sausages. Rationing in general was fair. And babies, of course, they had to have what was called National Dried Milk, and they thrived, were bonny. Orange juice they had and cod liver oil. Nobody starved so long as you used your common sense and didn't eat all your rations in the first couple of days.'

Lita Chivers, from Kingsmead Street, remembers how those who were part of a large family enjoyed certain economies of scale when it came to food rationing:

The shop frontages in Burton Street have changed little in 80 years, but the retailers are of a very different character today.

'If you were of a big family you came off better by pooling everything, and if you visited anyone you always took a little bit of your rations so as not to pull on anyone else's resources.' But the triumph in obtaining a rare fruit like the banana and the ceremonial sharing of it around the family is clearly recalled by Lita: 'I remember the first banana we had. I cut it into six portions so we could all have a taste. I think I queued for an hour for it!'

Margo Cogswell's mother was expecting Margo's sister:

'For this reason, she had a green ration book that allowed her bananas and you could go to the front of the queue to get them. People were swapping coupons. Towards the end of the war I can remember going down Westgate Street one day and everyone I could see was running, "Come! Come!" they were shouting, "Walshaw's is open and they've just made some ice cream!' I didn't know what ice cream was, so I had my first taste of it!'

The Cogswells had a big garden and part of a field next to their house in Hensley Road:

Eager shoppers queue for bananas in front of Lawrence's the greengrocer's, at 1 Burton Street. Rationing was still in force when this photograph was taken on 6 February 1946, although as a scene it is virtually indistinguishable from the dreary ration queues of the war years. (*Nora Bishop*)

'I used to go round with daddy in a car and pick up the swill bins that were standing on the corners outside the Christopher Hotel [in High Street] and all the other hotels. All this would be brought home and boiled up into swill to feed the pigs. You were allowed to have half a pig to keep. Holloway's, the butchers, would come and slaughter it for you and you would keep half a pig in a salt bath that we had in the outside loo. You weren't allowed to keep much of it for some reason. The meat was horrible to eat because it was so salty. We also kept turkeys and chickens for eating to supplement our meat ration, and also for the eggs. My father did the slaughtering of the poultry. Daddy used to send me out with a basket of eggs to people in Egerton Road. He would tell me not to worry if people didn't have any money to pay me for them. We had some black-market butter.'

Soap rationing was introduced on 2 February 1942. Everybody was allowed four coupons for each four-week period and each coupon could be used for toilet soap, hard soap, soap powder and soap flakes. Phyllis Miles' husband, Arnold, had a friend who was a butcher:

'We were all right for meat. We also knew someone who worked in a sweetshop, so we were all right for sweets as well. My sister worked in a grocer's shop in Hereford, and she used to send us dried fruits and caster sugar and tea. And I remember getting very frustrated about soap. You couldn't get enough soap. So, my neighbour in Third Avenue used to exchange soap for tea. That was worse than going without butter.'

Where food rationing was concerned, it clearly paid to keep your friendships in good repair, as Christina Brooks also recalls:

'Mother always seemed to find some little extras, she had some very good friends. In one year, my father was told of a man who was fattening turkeys for Christmas. My father reserved one for us and the man asked him to save and bring him any food scraps we might have to help fatten up "Ernie", as our turkey was named. Giving the turkey a name was a great mistake. When Christmas Day came and this great treat was brought to the table, apparently I suddenly realised that this was Ernie and I refused to eat any of it!'

Percy Taylor, Pamela's father, was a partner in a sweet factory in Bristol:

'Rationing didn't affect us much because with my dad having the factory he had sweets, and sweets would talk! Mind you we didn't get a lot of stuff, but we got some, especially at the butchers, and butter and things. I had two aunts at Priston, and my dad's cousins had a farm, so we didn't do badly for chickens. I think we were healthier for the rationing – I don't recall ever getting a cold during the war.'

Brian Hamilton, then living at Bathampton, remembers that rationing was a 'big chore':

'Running the village shop one would think we fared OK. But, in truth, we were worst off. We always had to have enough available to meet the rations, especially if soldiers returned home on leave, as they had priority – there was little to spare. Dried egg became quite a thing: it's

 There may have been a war on, but manufacturers were still keen to advertise their products. These hoardings at Ladymead in Walcot Street carry advertisements for a number of well-known wartime commodities: Craven Plain cigarettes, Germolene aseptic ointment, OXO 'on a plane by itself – ready and reliable', Whitbread's pale ale, and Exide batteries. There are also ads exhorting people to beware of fire bombs, and to save 'fuel for battle'.

surprising what you can grow to like! I remember when the father of one of my friends came home from sea and brought some bananas. My friend John took one to school and divided it between his gang. It was something I hadn't tasted for years. But the worst thing I remember about rationing was having to count the tiny coupons that had to be submitted to the Ministry of Food.'

Petrol, of course, was strictly rationed, and special allowances were made to those persons who needed extra supplies in order to carry on their profession or business. 'Tim' Cuppage's father, Dr Burke Cuppage, 'had to have enough to carry out his visits, but he was very conscientious – even giving up golf, thinking it was wrong to use the petrol for personal leisure.' That petrol rationing had drastically reduced the number of vehicles on the nation's roads was plain to see for Ivor Barnsdale one summer evening, when he 'cycled from Lansdown to Colerne, Chippenham, and back to Brunswick Place. In the whole time (3½ hours) I met not more than a dozen vehicles on the road!'

Clothes rationing began in June 1940. Lita Chivers was married the same year at St Saviour's Church, Larkhall:

'We had the reception at the Co-op in Westgate Buildings. It was 2/6d a head and I had sixty guests. I think the Government must have allowed rations to the various caterers for such events. I was lucky have good friends and family – they all gave me some of their clothing coupons to buy material for a white wedding dress. Later, when my husband and I got a house we were afforded dockets to buy certain items of furniture.'

When Ivor Barnsdale got married in June 1944, people still had to rely on gifts of clothing coupons from friends. New furniture was tightly rationed, but certain items were made available (on a rationed basis, of course) to newlyweds or to those who had been bombed out and who had lost everything. 'As for household items, furniture was of a standard "Utility" design and like clothes was also on coupons. We obtained a carpet, blankets etc., only by persistently inquiring at McIlroy's at the end of Bath Street. Most of our acquisitions were

'Make-do and mend' was a slogan never far from people's minds during the war. In common with food and other commodities, clothing was rationed. Although clothes bearing the 'Utility' standard mark were produced to a war economy standard, generally people made do with cut-me-downs and remodelled garments from the pre-war period.

In pre-war days, it was possible for the 'man-in-the-street' to purchase an off-the-peg suit for 50 shillings, when the average wage was about 56 shillings a week. The nationwide outfitters 'The Fifty Shilling Tailors' had two shops in Bath – both in Westgate Street – and they continued to supply suits at this price throughout the war and after.

The old-established firm of James Colmer in Union Street was eventually taken over by Owen and Owen, but the shop has long since closed its doors. With Jolly's in Milsom Street, it was for many years one of Bath's principal department stores. This Colmer's advertisement includes the wartime 'Utility' standard mark of two cut 'cheeses'.

second-hand and from auction sales or house clearances.'
In 1939, memories of life on the Home Front during the First World War were still vivid in the minds of the older generation – only twenty-one years had elapsed since the Armistice had been signed. During that war the horrors of life at the Front did not impinge greatly on social life at home. But people generally must have had guilty feelings about enjoying themselves while men at the Front were being gassed and slaughtered in their thousands. To be sure, there were a number of Zeppelin raids on London and on some provincial

towns and cities causing fear and general anxiety among the population. The Second World War, however, brought its horrors literally into the lives of the people at home who now felt that they shared many of the dangers of warfare with men and women serving in the Forces. There was an underlying anxiety in the population as a whole and the ever-present fear of gas attacks and air-raids made people realise that they were as vulnerable as those serving at the Front.

The great movements of population evacuees, servicemen and women and others – also brought instability into people's lives. This time, though, people felt that they could enjoy themselves without feelings of guilt. Taking part in social events of every kind became a form of escapism from the realities of war, and the authorities regarded such activities as morale boosters for people of all ages as they became worn down with war weariness and deprivation.

At the outbreak of war, cinemas and theatres were closed for a brief period because of the fear of mass casualties in the event of air-raids. But in time things soon settled down and places of public entertainment were reopened. Social events of all kinds proliferated – beetle drives and whist drives, dances and concerts, sports and so on. Throughout the war in Bath there were Saturday night dances at the Pavilion, Pump Room and Assembly Rooms, variety shows at the Palace Theatre and plays at the Theatre Royal. Movies were screened at the city's cinemas – the

The Pump Room Orchestra. Keeping up morale was of the utmost importance in wartime Britain. Concerts, recitals, and dances were popular and they provided a temporary respite from the realities of war.

Beau Nash, Forum, Odeon, Little Theatre and at the Scala in Moorland Road.

Mary James was too young to go to dances, but she went to the pictures and, following the Blitz, played tennis at Southdown Tennis Club where there were five grass courts. The Club was situated close to what is now St Alphege's church. Before the church in King Edward Road was built, Sunday worship was held in a 'tin hut' at the end of Junction Road where, during the winter months, she belonged to the youth club.

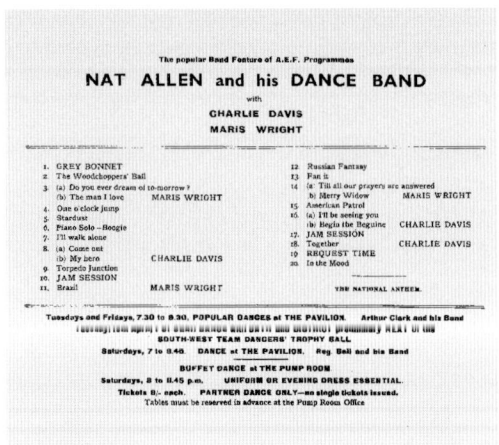

Weekly dances were held at the Pump Room, the Pavilion, and the Assembly Rooms with tickets at special prices for members of the Armed Forces. Among the favourite wartime bands that played in the city were the Squadronnaires, the Sky Rockets, and Nat Allen and his Dance Band. There were also the local bands of Arthur Clarke and Reg Ball.

'Tim' Cuppage remembers the enjoyment she had in the company of friends during the holidays in Bath – she was away at boarding school during term time.

> 'We played tennis at Lansdown in the Easter and summer holidays, went out on bikes, went to the cinema a lot – the Scala in Oldfield Park had two big films a week: Monday to Wednesday, and Thursday to Saturday. We listened avidly to the radio – ITMA being a great favourite. Jack Train who played 'Colonel Chinstrap' lived in Bath and, I believe, was partial to a drink!'

Eileen Rogers, then also in her teens, went out once a week (her father was quite strict) to the Pavilion, 'the meeting place for all the air force around. The Americans near Warminster used to flock to Bath at weekends.' During the winter months she listened to the radio. Her father also used to play the piano when he was off duty and the family would gather round and sing:

> 'During the blackout you couldn't go anywhere without your torch. At the cinema the news items were very popular – Pathé News – because it was our only visual contact with what was going on in the war. The Forum was our favourite cinema because it was the newest, we thought it quite palatial. The Scala was our little local one, which was alright and it had a balcony. But if you were really going to the cinema you had to go into Bath and the Forum. We did live it up – we really enjoyed it! You could forget about the war – it was all lit up inside and all black outside. The servicemen respected you, there was no pressurising from them. It was the highlight of the week to go to the Pavilion, and if you got a date then, well that was a bonus!'

Phyllis Miles came to Bath in 1940. Originally from South Wales, she met Arnold, her future husband, while in domestic service at Berrington Hall near Hereford. Arnold worked for a nursery outside Hereford, but unemployment brought him to Bath to seek work. He found a job at Walters Engineering in Stuart Place, and later at Stothert & Pitt's Victoria Works and Weston Island. Phyllis followed him to Bath where she found work at Horstmann's in Chelsea Road in June 1940. She remembers her nights out:

> 'When I first came to Bath I thought it was really beautiful, with plenty of entertainment, good company, and lots of dances going on. We used to go to all the dances at the Assembly Rooms, the Pump Room, and the Forum. Also to the theatre – the Palace, where all kinds of reviews and quite a lot of well-known artistes used to come down. The Assembly Rooms was the best – dance bands like Oscar Rabin, Henry Hall, Victor Sylvester – although those were "one-offs" on special occasions. I never went to any of the dances out in the country, but my husband went to Southdown and to Bristol, but that was before I came to Bath.'

Joan Barlow was billeted with other Admiralty colleagues at a hostel somewhere in Weston Park.

> 'The hostel provided company for people of similar ages. Sometimes we would go to the Pump Room where dances were held in both ballrooms. On Sundays, we went walking in the country, but signposts had been removed for the war and it was quite a challenge to find our way – none of us was local. We also enjoyed tennis, netball, horse-riding, theatre and concerts.'

Band leader Nat Allen and his musicians were from London. After the war they were a fixture at Ciro's Club just off London's Haymarket and also toured in Europe.

Pamela Taylor and a friend enjoyed roller-skating at the Pavilion. Pamela's father always met them afterwards because 'he didn't like us going with the airmen who were up at Colerne'. She was also a member of the Red Aces, a concert party (most of whom were from the Admiralty) that visited the RAF station at Colerne and other bases in the area. Pamela used to sing popular songs of the day like 'Cherry Ripe' and 'There'll Always be an England'.

Pat Bankart and her mother used to attend services at the Abbey where one of the curates was the Reverend Leslie ('Pooh') Hamilton Whiteside. He encouraged young people to join the Abbey Youth Club. 'We enjoyed life to the full in those days with river picnics, "Bun" parties and dances – lots of fun – cementing new friendships.' Pat recalls:

> 'Many of us met daily for coffee at Fortt's Restaurant in Milsom Street. We also fire-watched in the Abbey belfry. On one occasion, a group of us had been to a dance at the Victoria Rooms in Bristol. Having left late, we were unable to get transport back to Bath, so we decided to walk – myself barefooted and carrying my shoes! With practically no traffic on the road I arrived home about 3am to be met

FOOD, FUN AND CHEWING GUM

English girls enjoy a dance with American GI's 'somewhere in England'. Bath was no different from other English cities in its popular resentment of this 'friendly invasion'. Many of its young men subscribed bitterly to the view that the Yanks were 'over-paid, over-sexed and over here'.

by a very angry father! A group of us also used to attend the weekly Saturday night dances at the Assembly Rooms and the Pump Room.'

Trevor Canham's five-and-a-half days a week job with Underwood & Sons, the quantity surveyors, 'yielded a meagre salary', but with a small allowance from his parents he managed to stay solvent.

'Money for public transport was rarely needed as I walked or cycled everywhere. Beer was 9d (4p) a pint, beans on toast at Biddy's snack bar (under the high pavement on the Paragon) was also 9d. Similar snacks at the Hole-in-the-Wall cost a penny or two more, with the advantage of better seating. (I was interested to see the charges there during a recent visit!) On rare occasions I would indulge in the luxury of a visit to the Little Theatre, or buy a jazz record from Duck, Son & Pinker. I also used to go on walks with friends.'

Frank Mawer and his girlfriend Dudu Morgan went to the 1941 New Year's Eve Ball at the Assembly Rooms. For the occasion he had borrowed a tail-coat 'because it was all tail-coats and half-a-crown a time at the Assembly Rooms'. On the Monday morning after the Blitz in 1942, they walked past the gutted Assembly Rooms and remembered dancing in the New Year there: 'Dudu burst into tears – she couldn't help it.'

Frank believes that 'lots of people in Bath had decided that young chaps and young ladies ... needed some taking care of and things organised for them'. Among other things he was a keen rugby player and during his first winter in Bath played for a team known as 'The Exiles' – the Civil Service 'exiles', that is. They used to play on The Royal School playing field above Ensleigh.

Ivor Barnsdale, another young Admiralty employee, recalls that for a few weeks at the beginning of the war all places of entertainment were closed, but then cinemas and theatres gradually began to open again:

'When it was realised that the hundreds of Admiralty staff had no opportunity for social life, the church authorities turned over the upper floors of Abbey Church House to the Admiralty as a social club that opened from 6–10pm Monday to Friday, and from 2–10pm on Saturdays and Sundays. We had various committees including one for entertainment, of which I was in charge. It was known that I was a violinist and so I joined a concert party called "The Guinea Pigs" (after the guinea we paid our "billetors"). But soon the producer was moved and I was invited to take over. Subsequently, I obtained approval to form an official Admiralty concert party.

> We visited every Army, Navy and Air Force unit within 50
> miles of Bath – most of the time in the blackout. We gave
> about 300 concerts in all, including two in the Theatre Royal for charity.'

In the early part of the war, Miss Consuela De Reyes, of Citizen House next to the Little Theatre, decided to form a Little Theatre Club. Performances of plays were given on Sunday afternoons. Frank Mawer remembers Miss De Reyes, who was married to Peter King, as 'a delightful person'. The first play they performed was Thornton Wilder's Our Town. Frank, an acting member of the Club, recalls that it was the most hectic performance he gave: he 'had to jump into different costumes and put on different accents'. Later, he was given the lead in Potbound, a one-act play they presented in 1940. This particular play also provided Frank with romance. 'I saw a "vision" on the other side of the room with bobbing curls all over her head.' And that is how he met Miss Morgan, his wife-to-be. But it was to be some years before they were able to marry.

One day early in the war, Miss De Reyes asked Frank and his friend Jimmy Knight (son of the owner of the decorating shop in Bath Street) if they would take two of the girls then on her drama course to a Saturday evening dance at the Pump Room, with all expenses paid. They agreed. Frank's partner was called Ann Wrapson, while Jim's was a young lady who later became 'quite a stage celebrity'. After the dance was over, and as instructed, they took the girls back to the King's home, Doric House at Sion Hill, where they had been left coffee and plates of sandwiches. However, the two young men had been told not to stay too long! 'I remember these two girls with their long evening frocks. Quite suddenly the other girl – the actress to be – sat down at the piano and played and sang Schubert's Ave Maria. It has haunted me ever since.'

In 1940, the year following his arrival in Bath, Ivor Barnsdale, a violinist, joined Bath Choral and Orchestral Society that rehearsed in the Treatment Centre next to the old Grand Pump Room Hotel (now Arlington House).

> 'I remember we were preparing for Hiawatha's Wedding Feast.
> The other organisation was the Bath Philharmonic Orchestra, which
> rehearsed on Saturday afternoons in the canteen of Bayer's corset
> factory on the Lower Bristol Road near the Old Bridge. Mr Ernest
> Monk, the conductor, and his family were bombed out of Burlington
> Street and he did not restart the orchestra until late in 1943.'

For over two years from the outbreak of war, Britain and her Empire stood alone in opposing the armed might of the Third Reich. Britain's ally, France, fell to the German invaders in June 1940 and the French Government was exiled in London for the duration. Italy declared war on Britain that same month. In December 1941, following the unprovoked Japanese air attack on the United States naval base at Pearl Harbor in the Pacific, America, with her vast resources entered the war. It was not long before troopships crammed with American GIs began arriving in British ports.

The city of Bath was introduced to American servicemen as early as the late summer of 1942. Most were young men straight out of high school or first year at college and were youthful enough to be attracted to 16- or 17-year-old English girls. For many of these young Americans it was their first experience of the opposite sex. And for young and impressionable English girls, whose only knowledge of America was through the rose-tinted lens of Hollywood movies, the friendly exuberance of the 'Yanks' was often irresistible.

In 1942, the Lansdown Grove Hotel was requisitioned as an American Red Cross Services Club for enlisted and non-commissioned men in the US Army visiting Bath. There was also an American officers' club in the Royal Crescent. Phyllis Miles, who lived at Spencers Belle View on Lansdown Road, remembers the Americans at the nearby Lansdown Grove.

'My two younger sisters had a great time then because they met them quite a lot when they used to come and stay with us.' Brian Hamilton, who lived at Bathampton, remembers that the Americans were 'brash, with plenty of money and food'. Brian and other boys were entertained by the Americans at the Lansdown Grove. 'It was all the rage to ask for chewing-gum – often we would chase a lorry full of American GIs to get a stick of gum.'

American servicemen were generally resented by Englishmen whose girlfriends (and sometimes wives) were often enticed by their money and gifts of cigarettes, nylons, chocolate and chewing-gum. Eileen Wiggins remembers girls at the Co-op in Widcombe Parade where she worked, coming into the shop in the morning after a night out showing off their nylon stockings and saying, 'Look, look what I got last night!' And the girls who smoked used to say, '... all right, I got some Camel cigarettes'.

'Tim' Cuppage remembers that at weekends they had 'a delightful sergeant called Don Brennen who came for meals and a chat, and always brought "goodies" – canvas bags of sugar, and huge tins of fruit. Sometimes when out on our bikes, lorries of GIs went by and they would chuck out candy and tins of fruit for us.' Boys (and girls) who met Americans walking in the town would often ask, 'Got any gum, chum?'

WARTIME BATH: LIFE ON THE HOME FRONT 1939-45

Eileen Rogers, whose father James was a Bath policeman, recalled:

'When the Americans were here, they had their own military police. They wore white hats and were called "snowdrops". They looked after their own men and they had a special cell at Bath police station where they could take troublesome American servicemen. It was entirely under their jurisdiction.

'One Saturday night a couple of these "snow drops" brought in two American servicemen who were absolutely blotto and one of them was getting the better of the policeman, so dad and another

 Winning hearts and minds: US Army Military Policemen, Guy and Joe, chat to Phyllis Mossman and young family friend Peter Reeves in the Circus. Phyll lived with her mother and grandmother at 20 Brock Street. Their home was among many that suffered damage in the Blitz. Notice the grimy facades of the houses.

144

policeman went to his aid. But this drunk American got dad's hand in his mouth, clamped on it, and broke two bones ... and to the day he died, he still had those puncture marks. Because the American was so drunk, they couldn't do anything with him.'

Muriel Elmes recalls that American servicemen were 'disliked very much by English soldiers'. The cause seems to have been that the Americans had a great deal more money than the average 'Tommy' and tended to flaunt it in front of them. There were frequent fights in public houses as a result. Early in 1943, it was Dr Ted Matthews' considered opinion that:

'It would be ridiculous to say that American troops are unpopular here. There are plenty about, but in spite of all sorts of efforts nobody seems to have met any Americans. Organised hospitality is rather obviously a mistake and I am not surprised that Americans avoid it, but personal contact, personal invitations and friendly conversations, surely these things ought to be possible.'

With the war's end, American servicemen returned home across the Atlantic to pick up their lives 'stateside'. Some took with them English brides to start a new life in what many saw as the land of plenty and opportunity, a world away from war weary Britain. Kathleen Clemas, who worked for the Admiralty at the Empire Hotel, met her future husband at the Civil Service Badminton Club, of which both were members:

'I married an American named Lawrence F. Cameron who at that time was a sergeant in the US Army Air Force stationed at Keevil airfield [near Trowbridge]. Our marriage was on 6 February 1944, at St Stephen's church, Lansdown. My son was born at the Royal United Hospital in 1945, but my husband had already been sent overseas by then. It wasn't until April 1946 that I was able to sail to America as one of the War Brides, and my husband saw his one-year-old son for the first time. I have lived here happily ever since, although my husband died in 1974. I still retain my British citizenship.'

The Yanks might have gone home, but in postwar Britain rationing was there to stay for several more years. In fact, it got worse because bread (unrationed in wartime) went on ration for two years in 1946 and the return to normality was a long time in coming. Clothing rationing did not end until 1949, and petrol rationing in the following year.

CHAPTER 8
TOWARDS VICTORY

Many Bath people have memories of isolated incidents during the war that excited them. Phyllis Miles and her husband remember going out one evening for a drink at the Jubilee Inn below Twerton Roundhill. Suddenly, a German plane flew over: 'even though the siren hadn't gone. It started dropping bombs over Pennyquick and we dived into a hedge.' David Falconer, who lived in Brunswick Place, recalls that:

'One morning quite early, as the Corsham workers were walking along Julian Road and Montpelier to catch their bus at the bottom of Guinea Lane, a German aircraft appeared from the western end of Julian Road and machine-gunned the men in the street. Taken completely by surprise, they jumped into doorways to take shelter. It was all over in a matter of seconds. Apparently, no one was injured. Shrapnel marks could still be seen in walls many years afterwards.'

On another occasion, a German aircraft flew low over the house from the direction of Batheaston. 'I ran to the window at the back of the house and saw the plane fly over the Circus trees in the direction of Twerton Roundhill. I could see the cockpit and the markings quite clearly.'

For many Bathonians, to see an enemy aircraft skimming the rooftops of their city was a symbolic reminder of why they were at war. Others had a far closer brush with the enemy, and virtually on their own front doorstep. After they moved to a new home in Third Avenue, Phyllis and Arnold Miles became used to seeing 'a bus-load of German prisoners go up every day to lay foundations for the prefabs in Hillside Road'. Valerie Ford also remembers how she and her younger brother 'would go and watch the roads being made by German prisoners-of-war on

Insignia swapped by German prisoners-of-war with Valerie Ford and her brother for sugar and cocoa. (*Valerie Gay*)

The Moorfields estate (pictured in 2001) was one of the first social housing developments to be built in Bath. During its construction, Valerie Ford and her brother used to watch the roads being made by German POWs who were brought every day by coach from Thorny Pits in Wiltshire. In return for cocoa and sugar, the prisoners sometimes gave the children buttons, badges and stripes from their uniforms. Some prisoners chose to remain in Britain after the war was over and a few married local girls. (*Authors/Valerie Gay*)

the Moorfields council estate. They would come daily by coach from Thorny Pits, Wiltshire. We would take sugar and cocoa to them and they would tear a button, badge or stripes off their uniforms in return.' Up at Whiteway Circle, Betty Cottle recalls how 'over the field at the back there was this hedge behind where they had prisoners-of-war working. My sister seemed to think they had a big mark on their backs, a yellow cross or something. They used to work in this field, a turnip field. It's now Blagdon Park, off Haycombe Drive.'

During the war the ringing of church bells was forbidden, except in the event of invasion. But special dispensation was often given for bells to be rung in celebration of Allied victories as they occurred. Hylton Bayntun-Coward used to walk up North Road to St Christopher's School. 'One day I heard the sound of church bells – presumably on the radio. As this had been the signal that the Germans had landed, I covered the remaining half-mile in record time!'

Bellringers and fire-watchers pose for the camera outside the belfry on the Abbey's roof on 15 November 1942, after the first peel to be rung since the Dunkirk evacuation two years earlier.

Mr Joe Woodward, who lived on the Warminster Road, regularly organised tours of the city by the Bathampton Scout Troop to celebrate particular victories. It was in connection with the Allied landing at Sicily in July 1943 that the photograph below was taken in Stall Street.

By early 1944, it was evident that the tide of war had turned decisively in the Allies' favour. Dr Ted Matthews, writing late one night in April that year, ended his letter with these evocative words: 'I really must go to bed, it is 11.30pm. The sky is full of aircraft, droning away up in the darkness as it is every night of the week. Thank heaven they are ours!'

In common with many other young boys of the time, David Falconer, then aged 10, followed the events during the latter days of the war with keen interest. In 1944, as preparations were being made for the invasion of Normandy, he remembers Henderson (the Falconers' billetee) telling them after an official visit to Weymouth that 'something big' was about to happen. He said that all the roads leading into Weymouth were filled with lines of military vehicles, and that he had passed through a number of military checkpoints.

Operation 'Overlord' – the Allied invasion of northwest Europe – had been meticulously planned for some time and on the eve of 6 June the great invasion force got underway. Patricia Bankart, a Bath girl

 'Sicily Victory Completed (official)' reads the placard in this Bathampton Scout Troop victory parade along Stall Street in July 1943. The parades were organised by Mr Joseph Woodward who lived in Warminster Road. Brian Hamilton recalled that 'he had us going around Bath early in the mornings showing the John Bull spirit!'. Outriders: Roy Dolman John Barrof, Brian Hamilton. Seated with Stars & Stripes: Paul Westcott, David Chapman (John Bull). The riders are led by Mr Woodward. (*Brian Hamilton*)

then serving in the WAAF at No 10 Group Headquarters (Combined Operations), was able to observe the huge movement of men, vehicles and aircraft, at first hand:

> 'To watch the movements of the three services leaving the north of the UK and going south by land, sea, and air, was a thrilling experience. I am still proud of having been able to take a small part in that intensive operation. The atmosphere in the "ops" room was electric. No one could persuade me to take a break – I wasn't going to miss anything. It was an emotional time.'

But victory was still some way off and there would be setbacks as well as gains before the German Fatherland eventually fell to the overwhelming military and industrial might of the Allies. When Victory in Europe was officially announced on 8 May 1945, church bells all over the country rang out in joyful peals, and relieved families celebrated with street parties, amid the realisation that husbands, brothers and sweethearts still on active service would soon be home again.

Pat Bankart (later Pat Woods) in WAAF uniform. She recalled that while on duty at RAF Turnhouse, Edinburgh, 'we plotted the arrival of a lone German aircraft. It turned out to be the one piloted to Scotland by Rudolf Hess on his ill-fated mission. There was a sense of amazement and speculation about the purpose of his unexpected arrival.' (Pat Woods)

Valerie Ford recalls how, on VE-Day, the residents of Coronation Avenue celebrated with a neighbour bringing her piano outside for singing and dancing in the street. 'My mother, Olive Ford, who was a teacher of singing, stood in the road and sang "Land of Hope and Glory".' Daisy Baker, who lived in Upper Bloomfield Road, remembers how 'we just went mad! I can remember trying to get up to the Burnt House. We just walked around and around and around, and kissed everybody.'

After four years' service in the Far East, it was customary for British troops to be repatriated for a month's home leave, then often they were sent off again to the war front. Phyllis Bond's soldier husband, a tank driver in the Prince of Wales' Own 3rd Dragoon Guards, happened to be home on 'repat leave' when the end of the war in Europe was declared. She recalls:

> 'Twerton had a street party in the High Street, just singing and dancing, but mostly, of course, it was civilians. It was bitter-sweet for us because the worst war zone of the lot was still going full blast. But they were the "forgotten army". We were still waiting for the atom

bombs to be dropped, those of us who'd men out there, and when that happened there was real rejoicing from all of us! I remember somebody, I don't know who, got up an impromptu concert in the Victoria Park round the bandstand, complete with a band. Before it started, the unknown MC said "we are now going to start with songs from the war before the last". A big groan went up until suddenly the penny dropped – the war was completely over. "Tipperary" and the songs we'd expected were from the war before the last. We really could believe the long nightmare was over at long last.'

 Victory in Europe 1945. Flags displayed by the shops in Milsom Street. On the left of the picture is the shop of John R. Huntley & Son, the provision merchants. Above the houses in Edgar Buildings (top centre) can be seen the huge sign advertising Evans & Owen's shop in Bartlett Street. (*Eric Lanning*)

Relief and rejoicing, though, were tinged with inconsolable sadness for those individuals and families who had lost loved ones in the terrible conflict: they would never come home again. David Falconer remembers one such instance in the neighbourhood of Lansdown Road. 'We habitually bought our greengroceries at Bailey's shop in Belvedere, where two of the assistants were Mr and Mrs Scott. Their son was in the Royal Navy and the ship on which he was serving was sunk. For many months the Scotts had no word as to his fate. They were a sad couple, always

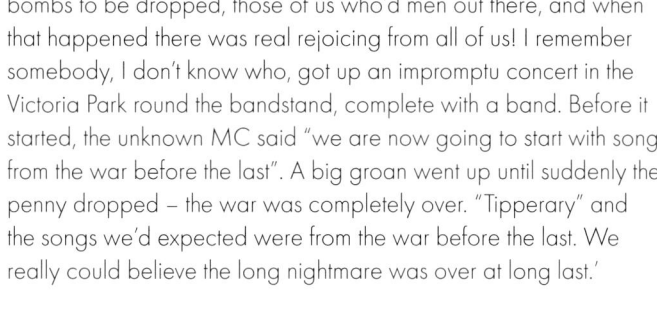

preoccupied with their thoughts. Eventually the dreaded news came through: a telegram telling them their son was missing "presumed killed". He was their only child. Such was the fate of so many parents in wartime.'

Ray Burgess, a Bath fireman, spent VE-Day working in the fire station workshops at Cleveland Bridge. He finished work at 5 o'clock having heard the victory news at midday. 'But after midday we celebrated. I was a bit the worse for wear by the time I got home to Faulkland Road. It was a hot sunny day. The best place was on the lawn with my cap over my face. Audrey wouldn't have me indoors!'

At Whiteway Circle, Betty Cottle and her neighbours had organised a big street party:

> 'It was a lovely party, and I can remember Mr Bidwell, the next-door neighbour, because most of his family are now in Canada – they all emigrated. We had this lovely party with dancing. We had these coloured lights up in the bedroom, it was a super time. My elder sister and one of the older girls from another family went round to people's houses to see what they could collect to make things for the party. I can remember this great big enamel jug they took with them to collect vinegar in, but all they came back with was a tiny bit. A few days after, we all dressed up in costume and walked from Haycombe Drive down The Hollow, down Lansdown View, over to Station Road leading up

St Martin's Hospital at Combe Down was extended to receive the wounded of the Great War. During the Second World War, more than 200 victims of the Bath Blitz were treated here, as well as servicemen injured in North Africa and Normandy, who also spent time convalescing in the peaceful surroundings. Here, a group of patients pose with medical staff on VJ-Day. (Bob White)

The war in the Far East was finally brought to an end by the two atom bombs dropped on Hiroshima and Nagasaki in August 1945. The official VJ-Day was on 15 August. With the war in Europe over, victory celebrations in Britain were muted: people had done enough celebrating – they just wanted to get on with their lives. In this picture, flags can be seen flying in Union Street in celebration of VJ-Day. (*Eric Lanning*)

to Chelsea Road, and right out to Weston village and collected money for Alkmaar. My sister said we collected £40 for the twin town to Bath.'

Civil Servant Kathleen Clemas had married American airman Lawrence Cameron in February 1944. In late April 1945, Kathleen was in the Royal United Hospital where her son was born. 'In those day they kept the mothers in hospital for two weeks and so on 8 May I was still there. Another mother and I got up and went over to the ward windows to watch the fireworks, until the matron walked in and sternly ordered us back to bed! So passed my Victory in Europe Day!' For Grace Selley, who lived on Combe Down, VE-Day rejoicing also brought with it the safe return home of her husband, Victor, from active service overseas. 'I always remember the day before when he wrote to say that he had landed in Liverpool, and hoped to be home to join the celebrations. The next thing I knew was when his taxi drew up outside the door.'

'This is your victory': Winston Spencer Churchill, the wartime premier, gives his celebrated 'V' for victory sign.

For Muriel Elmes, a Bath schoolteacher, the VE-Day celebrations reminded her that the war was over at last, and there was no longer any need to put up the blackout:

> 'We could walk the streets in safety once more and go to our beds again without fear. For the first time in their lives, small children, not quite six years old, could run about freely and happily. To sum it up: I remember how much enjoyment and happiness the many street parties gave to all, no matter whether they were participants or onlookers.'

Now that almost 80 years separates us from that time, it is hard to imagine the wonderful feeling of relief felt by everyone. When Eileen Rogers saw the lights come on again, she felt it was 'absolutely something':

> 'We lived in Englishcombe Lane, and from the back of our house you could look right over to Bath and see it all lit up. It was wonderful not to have the ritual of putting up the blackout every night, and making sure. And the funny thing, during those six years, because there were no streetlights or lights in the houses, we didn't see any flying insects in the summer time. This was 8 May and we were all dancing around the streetlight outside our house, and to our horror these horrible maybugs were buzzing around the light. Where they'd been during the war I don't know, but they suddenly appeared. When I went to work on that day hardly any work was done: you felt as though everything had lifted and it was a lovely feeling.'

Writing on 17 August 1945, two days after Emperor Hirohito announced the surrender of Japanese forces to the Allies, Dr Ted Matthews found that 'the relaxation of strain did not come with VE-Day as we hoped it would. The mood did not change in spite of the rejoicings.' And, of course, for those with loved ones who had been fighting the 'forgotten war' in the Far East, there was little to celebrate just yet. Their victory celebrations would have to wait until their menfolk finally returned home, as Phyllis Bond remembers:

> 'It took a long time for the men to be demobbed, but I can truthfully say that was my happiest moment, meeting my husband off the train – he was wearing an ill-fitting suit, trilby hat, shirt, tie and shoes. Being from overseas they had to go first to Taunton, the county town, to be discharged. I think it was £36 gratuity money for six year's active service. I can't remember if he brought his uniform home, but I do know he had his black Royal Tank Regiment beret and 14th Army badge.'

The happiness experienced by Phyllis in accepting that the war was finally over and that her husband had come safely home to her, is a fitting finale to this story of Bath's war on the home front. 'I can't even remember what day it was,' she recalls. 'It seemed such a long time coming. Our seventh wedding anniversary was the first we'd spent together.'

ACKNOWLEDGEMENTS

The authors would like to thank the following individuals and organisations for their help in the research and writing of this book:

Barry Cruse, Nigel Gillard, for the loan of various wartime issues of the *Bath Chronicle*; Bill Hanna, for his help in compiling the Roll of Honour; Colin Johnston, Bath City Archivist; Graham Payne for putting us in touch with several interviewees; John Penny for allowing us to refer to his unpublished dissertation 'Bath: The most devastating Baedeker Blitz'; Jim Warren, Bath Blitz Memorial Project, for kind permission to quote copyright material; Dr Kenneth Lee, for kindly allowing us to quote from his late father's war memoir, *1939-45: Evacuation to Bath*; Rod Suddaby and Ann Brooks of the Department of Documents at the Imperial War Museum, London. We are particularly grateful to Ann for spending the best part of a day with us going through the Matthews-Meem letters; and the Matthews family for their generous permission to quote from them; Margaret Paroutaud (née Haynes) and Kathleen Teece (née Seers) for allowing us to use extracts from their war memoirs; C.A. Bastin, Nora Bishop, Mark Coath-Wilson, David Crellin, Robin Mumme, Neil Short, Rose Scriven, John Venn and Bridget Wakefield for permission to reproduce photographs in their possession; and Rose Scriven for kindly allowing us to quote from a letter written by her father.

Thanks are also due to the following organisations for permission to reproduce copyright material from their collections: the Trustees of the Imperial War Museum, for permission to quote extracts from letters and other documents in their collections (full details of which can be found at the end of this book in the list of sources); the Victoria Art Gallery, Bath; Bath Reference Library; the *Bath Chronicle*; Solihull Mobile Library Headquarters; Aerofilms Ltd; the *Illustrated London News*; Nick McCamley at Folly Books, for kind permission to quote an extract from *Salute to the Village* by Fay Inchfawn.

And last but not least, the interviewees, who welcomed us into their homes and whose help, enthusiasm and cooperation we gratefully acknowledge:

Daisy Baker, Joan Barlow, Ivor Barnsdale, Hylton Bayntun-Coward, Freda Beatty, Phyllis Bond, Christina Brooks, Ray and Audrey Burgess, Kathleen Cameron (née Clemas), Trevor Canham, John Coe, Lita Elliott (née Chivers), Muriel Elmes, R.C. Fry, Terence Gay, Valery Gay (née Ford), Margot Gliddon (née Cogswell), Keith Gover, Brian Hamilton, Joan Hurford, Aubrey Jackman, Mary James, Raymond Jones, Eric Lanning, Betty Ludlow (née Cottle), 'Dudu' Mawer (née Morgan), Frank Mawer, 'Tim' Molly McConnell (née Cuppage), Phyllis Miles, Ted Peters, Joan Potter, R.J. 'Rocky' Rochester, Eileen Rosevear (née Rogers), Eileen Millard (née Wiggins), Grace Selley (née Wiggins), Pat Simmonds, Sylvia Weeks (née Hancock), Pamela Voysey (née Taylor), Bob White, Freda Whittern, Basil Williams, Pat Woods (née Bankart).

BIBLIOGRAPHY AND LIST OF SOURCES

PRIMARY SOURCES – documentary
Bath City Archives
WW2 Boxes – Bath City Council Records: Air Raid Incidents and Occurrences, 1940–42

Bath Reference Library
R7/9432 (B 012.38) Diary of Miss Sidney Lloyd, 19 Park Lane, Bath – 1940–43

Commonwealth War Graves Commission
Register of War Dead website – www.cwgc.org

Imperial War Museum
Department of Documents
Ref: 86/5/1 – Mrs M.D. Paroutaud (Margaret Haynes), typescript memoir
MISC 180, Item 2730 – photocopied booklet of short memories including article by Kathleen Teece
Ref: 10499 – letters of Dr and Mrs E. Matthews to their daughters in USA, 1940–44

Sound Archive
Ref: 28637 – Selford, Alison Flora, oral history (recorded 12 Oct 2005)

Public Record Office, Kew
AIR27/1025 – 152 Squadron Operations Record Book

Private sources
Dr Sammy Marle – letter

PRIMARY SOURCES – oral history interviews
Carried out during 2000–2001 – Daisy Baker, Joan Barlow, Ivor Barnsdale, Hilton Bayntun-Coward, Freda Beatty, Phyllis Bond, Christina Brooks, Ray and Audrey Burgess, Kathleen Cameron, Trevor Canham, John Coe, Lita Elliott, Muriel Elmes, Valerie Ford, R.C. Fry, Terence Gay, Margo Gliddon, Keith Gover, Brian Hamilton, Joan Hurford, Aubrey Jackman, Mary James, Raymond Jones, Eric Lanning, Betty Ludlow, 'Dudu' Mawer, Frank Mawer, 'Tim' (Molly) McConnell, Phyllis Miles, Ted Peters, Joan Potter, R.J. 'Rocky' Rochester, Eileen Rosevear, Eileen Millard, Grace Selley, Pat Simmonds, Pamela Voysey, Bob White, Freda Whittern, Basil Williams and Pat Woods.

Carried out in October 2021 – Sylvia Weeks.

SECONDARY SOURCES – published books
Ede, Mary, *Bath High School 1875–1998*
'Impresario', *The Market Square: The Story of the Food Ration Book 1940–1944* (London, HMSO, 1944)
Inchfawn, Fay, *Salute to the Village* (2010, Folly Books)
Rothnie, Niall, *The Baedeker Blitz* (1992, Ian Allan Ltd)

Newspapers
Bath & Wilts Chronicle & Herald, various issues for the war years, 1939–45

Pamphlets
Air Raid Precautions: Official Guide to the Civil Defence Services (Bath City Council, 1941)

SECONDARY SOURCES – unpublished dissertation
Penny, John, 'Bath: The Most Devastating Baedeker Blitz', (Bath Spa University College, 1998)

Recollections
Lee, Eric, '1939–1945: Evacuation to Bath' (Bath City Council, typescript, n.d.)

SECONDARY SOURCES – Internet
Bath Blitz Memorial Project – http://www.bathblitz.org

APPENDIX 1
BATH'S WAR DEAD

CIVILIANS KILLED BY ENEMY ACTION 1939–45
Below are listed the names of civilians killed in Bath during the Second World War by enemy action. The names of 34 members of the Home Guard, Police, AFS, Civil Defence, Medical Service workers and military personnel who were killed on active service in the city during the Baedeker Blitz on 25–27 April 1942 can be found listed in Appendix 2 on pages 161–162.

Twerton High Street, 16 January 1941 (6 killed)
Alexander Sealey Phillips, Doris Randall, Ellen Randall, Robert Randall, William George Rogers, William Frederick Weston.

The Dolemeads, Widcombe, 12 April 1941 (10 killed)
Mary Matilda Derrick, Elizabeth Gay, William Gay, Georgina Ann Lidgett, Robert Stanley Norris, Joe Dimery Seeke, Patricia Frances Sharman, Herbert Arthur Waterson, George William White, Phoebe White.

The 'Baedeker' Blitz, 25–27 April 1942 (374 killed)
First attack – 25/26 April (88 killed)
Doris Alcock, Harry Bertram Alcock, William Phillip Russell Bamford, Lydia Bowler, John Brannigan, Irene Ann Brewer, Sarah Brewer, Violet Alice Mary Brewer, Edward Joseph Broad, Dorothy Laura Brown, Charles Victor Norman Brown, Norman Victor Brown, Edgar Leonard Burden, Amelia Caroline Cutting, John Alfred Cutting, Norah Lilian Cutting, Terence Cutting, Amelia Mary Davis, Beatrice Mary Davis, George John Davis, June Mary Davis, Pamela Joan Davis, James Horseman Drague, Oliver Eagle, Frank Albert Ellis, Eliza Flower, Clifford Henry Ford, Cyril Alexander Ford, Frances Emily Ford, Frances Ethel Ford, Mavis Rose Ford, Ronald Dennis Ford, Thomas John Ford, William Philip Ford, Edith Greenland, Ellen Griffin, Francis Wyndham Griffin, Roy Chamberlain Gunstone, Kate Harris, Herbert Victor Hibberd, Thomas Hibberd, Ada Kate Hooper, Clara Mary Hooper, Helen Rose Hooper, Mabel Emma Hooper, Amy Lilian May Jefferies, Muriel Elizabeth Jefferies, Joyce Lambert, Gladys Leakey, Leonard Leakey, Mavess McKenzie, Frank William Martin, William Charles Mitchell, Isaac Nolan, John Noonan, Alfred Parker, Florence Ethel Parker, Kate Emmeline Parker, George Pease, Cyril Phillips, Ivy Lilian Preater, Clara Prescott, Ethel Rapsey, Margaret Patricia Rapsey, Rita Elizabeth Rosemary Rapsey, Bernard Oliver Patrick Reilly, James Hillman Ruddle, Florence Taylor Ryall, Queenie Alice Sell, Rolf Simons, Patrick Joseph Smyth, Ernest Spence, William Spurrell, Blanche Stone, Margaret Swatton, Ruby Swatton, Dorothy Winifred Vines, Frederick Vowles, Sarah Ann Watts, Susannah Watts, Ellen Madeline Emily Whitehead, Richard Williams, William Henry Woods, Eliza Wotton, Henry Wotton, Kate Emmelia Wotton, Leonard Wotton.

WARTIME BATH: LIFE ON THE HOME FRONT 1939-45

Second attack – 26 April (140 killed)

John Adams, Cyril Adkins, James Arkle, Harry Ashby, Ellen Louise Balsom, Edith Emily Bird, Albert Victor Blackwell, Hugh Brice, Janet Mary Brice, Veronica Brice, Beatrice Elizabeth Brown, Margaret Hilda Brown, Seymour Hanham Buckingham, Frederick Amos Canfield, Leonard Glynne Chapman, Lilian Gladys Chapman, Dorothy Lavinia Conroy, George Frederick James Cooper, Edith Fanny Dando, Annie Dean, Mary Henrietta Derrick, Thomas Elley, Alexander Franklyn, Margaret Elizabeth German, Elizabeth Giddings, Margaret Ann Goddard, Charles Henry Gooding, Eugenia Emma Gooding, Dora Louise Grace, Muriel Beatrice Grace, Audrey May Griffin, Doris Marian Grimshaw, Marian Grimshaw, Charles Arthur Gunstone, Royston Charles Gunstone, Albert Hancock, Daisy Beatrice Hancock, Rita Hancock, Emily Hardick, Hubert James Hardick, William Ewart Harris, June Edna Hart, John Hartley, Ernest James Hayter, Elsie Adelaide Horstmann, Percival Francis Horstmann, Terence Frederick Horstmann, George Frederick Hull, Hannah Charlotte Hull, Sylvia Joan Hull, Louisa Humphries, Alice Maud Hunt, Charles Henry Hunt, Ethel Lilian Hunt, Violet May Hunt, Lily May Hurford, Grace Emma Mary Hutchings, Daniel Jenkins, Kathleen Frances Johnson, Ivy Rosina Joyce, Mary Kilminster, Walter George Kilminster, Gladys King, Joyce Elizabeth King, Walter Alfred Lake, Dorothy Winifred Lambert, Edward John Lewis, Lily May Lewis, William George Long, William Mackey, Mary Elizabeth March, Phyllis Violet March, Constance Ellen Mabel Massey, Joseph Henry Massey, Leah Matilda Massey, Sarah Barnard Massey, Violet Matthews, Ellen G. Meedick, Henry Miles, Alfred Walter Miller, Alice Miller, Patrick Murray, Sheila May Neate, John O'Shea, Albert Oliver, Alice Oliver, Charles William Packwood, Leslie Padfield, Dorothy Evelyn Palk, Graham Palmer, Jesse Francis Parke, Ursula Jean Parke, William Edwin Parsons, Alma Eveline Poole, Florence Clara Poole, William Poole, Marjorie Olive Powell, Elizabeth Prescott, Joyce Prescott, Thomas Henry Prescott, Patricia Randall, Dora Pyles, Beatrice Rattray, Christine Rattray, Donald Rattray, George Rattray, Joan Rattray, Pamela Rattray, Shirley Rattray, William Rattray, William Frederick Rattray, Eric Bernard Reynaert, Evelyn May Reynaert, Ellen Jane Sellman, Gloria Ellen Kathleen Doreen Selman, Frederick William Slocombe, Janet Christine Smith, Lilian Nancy Smith, Margaret Nancy Smith, Ruby Smith, Brian Danny Taylor, Florence Maud Taylor, Frank Louis Taylor, Joyce Taylor, Maud Mary Taylor, Ivy Elsie Evelyn Theaker, Stanley Richard Tonkin, Nellie Rebecca Tucker, Orlando William Tucker, Elizabeth Hannah Verrier, Brian John White, Gertrude Alice Wilcox, Emily Frances Workman, Harold Tarrant Wright, Morwenda (Wendy) Wright, William John Wright, Bernice Brenda Young, Bertha Edith Young, Valerie Christine Young, Francis Cyril Young.

Third attack – 27 April (146 killed)

Gwenda Alton, Sidney L. Alton, Winnie Alton, Violet Arthurs, Albert Charles Bailey, Albert Edward Bailey, Doris May Bailey, Lilian Bailey, Freda Baker, John Beattie, Lorna Barbara Bell, Edith A. Beretford, Hubert Walter Bessant, Evelyn Bird, Gladys Bird, Cherry Amorelle Blackmore, Dorothy Amorelle Blackmore, Christopher James Breen, Frederick George Brewer, Frederick Bryant, Martha Annie Buckley, Catherine Caplin, Rachel Caulfield, Marion Clark, Bertha Clarke, Charles Neville Clarke, Sidney O'Connell Cormack, Catherine Eliza Cox, Oliver George Cox, Arthur James Curtis, Avril Jean Davies, Betty Eason, Lilian Eason, Richard Charles Eason, Herbert Victor Evans, Emily Frances Eyre, Ernest George Crocker Ferdinand, Violet Hilda Ferdinand, John Foody, Margaret Foody, Margaret Jane Gait, Fanny Heathcote Gale, Ethel Elizabeth Gamlin, Amelia George, Herbert Thomas George, Henry Goodman, Ellen Mary Gover, Gilbert Gover, Grace Gover,

Martin Grievson, Wilfred Henry Hatcher, Enid Hawkins, Amy Hayden, Violet Norah Hayden, Florence Elizabeth Hayward, Tom Belfield Hayward, Kenneth Alan Hill, Colin Edward Holmes, Prudence Mabel Holmes, Royston William Holmes, Frances James Leigh Howard, Maria Ethel Howard, Susan Ellen Johnson, Ellen Louise Jolliffe, Elsie Beatrice Jolliffe, Mary Eliza Jolliffe, Kate Elizabeth Medland, Alice Jones-Mitton, Phyllis May Northey Jones-Mitton, Catherine Keegan, Frances Rosa King, Leonard Henry Kingman, Margaret Kirkland, Sheila Mary Kirkland, Hilda Nellie Lagden, Edith Mary Sybil Langworthy, Lily Rosina Lewis, Margaret Annie Lichfield, Cissie Lieberman, Louisa Light, Mildred Light, Patricia Light, Anne McDonald, Mary Elizabeth Miles, Thomas George Mills, Robert J. Moffat, Charles Moody, Edward Rushforth Blakiston Murray, Hester Doreen Murray, Hilda Dorothea Murray, Albert Victor Neathey, Dorothy Nelson-Ward, Edith Augusta Beresford Oliver, Henry Ward Oliver, Jean Margaret Ollis, Reginald John Ollis, Alice Emma Oxford, Mary Packer, Cecil Pearson, May Evelyn Pearson, Emily Ada Perchard, Ada A. Perrett, Emily Perrett, Samuel Edward Perrett, Victor John Phillips, Constance Winifred Piercy, Alice Lily Pocock, Molly Pocock, Charles Price, William Pumphrey, Gilbert Robbins, Kate Adelaide Rossiter, Nella Constance Salter, Gertrude Sanson, Isabel Eleanor Louisa Shand, Timothy Sheridan, Norman Simmons, Henry Vincent Small, Kate Small, Annie Grace Smith, Frederick David Smith, Maureen Rachel Smith, Sidney Smith, Anthony Spence, Mary Spence, Agnes Genevieve Spurrell, Bernadette Agnes Sweet, Eileen Amelia Sweet, Emma Tanner, Audrey Ross Thomas, Reginald Percy Thomas, Emily Timmins, Florence Kate Weeks, Alfred Richard Augustus Wells, Minnie Wells, Eileen Wetterley, Royston Stanley White, Beatrice Maud Williams, Nora Kathleen Whitty, Jane Williams, Thomas Williams, Geoffrey Erskine Woodmansey, Eleanor Margaret Wilkinson, Maud Caroline Wilkinson, Frank Williamson, Clara Woodward.

APPENDIX 2
BATH'S WAR DEAD

KILLED ON ACTIVE SERVICE DURING THE BAEDEKER BLITZ, 25–27 APRIL 1942

Below are listed the names of thirty-four men and women who died in the Baedeker Blitz as a result of enemy action while serving with the Civil Defence Services. Of these, it has not been possible to provide the exact date of death of three men, so for the purpose of this list it is assumed that they died at some time during the period of the raids. Also included are the names of two RAF servicemen caught up in the raids, who were probably on leave.
at the time.

Adkins, F.H., Constable, Special Constabulary 26/04/42
Angus, C.W., Depot Superintendent, Civil Defence Service 26/04/42
Barrow, W.C.L., Constable, Special Constabulary 26/04/42
Bartlett, C.W., Senior Warden, Civil Defence Service 27/04/42
Blackmore, P.F., LAC RAFVR 28/04/42
Brown, F.A., F/S RAF 26/04/42
M.E.L. Coates, (Miss), Warden, Civil Defence Service 27/04/42
Coles, P.F.G., Pte 5 Som (Bath City) Bn HG 26/04/42

Davis, F.E., Sgt 5 Som (Bath City) Bn HG 26/04/42
Frapwell, H., Fire Guard, Civil Defence Service (exact date unknown)
Goddard, A., Warden, Civil Defence Service 26/04/42
Hayward, A., Sgt, Special Constabulary 26/04/42
G. Hooper, (Miss), Telephonist AFS 26/04/42
James, C.D., Constable, Special Constabulary 26/04/42
Jenkins, M., Constable, Special Constabulary (exact date unknown)
Kilminster, L.C., Pte 5 Som (Bath City) Bn HG 26/04/42
Lott, T., Constable, Special Constabulary 26/04/42
MacDougall, A., Warden, Civil Defence Service 27/04/42
E.B. Middlemas, (Miss), Casualty Service 27/04/42
M. Middlemas, Dr (Miss), Medical Officer, Casualty Service 27/04/42
Mills, T.L.G., Pte 5 Som (Bath City) Bn HG 26/04/42
Oatley, L., Warden, Civil Defence Service 27/04/42
Packwood, C.W., Inspector, Special Constabulary 26/04/42
Park, F.J., Pte 5 Som (Bath City) Bn HG 26/04/42
Parsons, C.W., Constable, Special Constabulary 26/04/42
Pearson, D.C., Pte 5 Som (Bath City) Bn HG 26/04/42
Pearson, H.G., Messenger Service (exact date unknown)
Perkins, A.M., Constable, Special Constabulary 26/04/42
Sales, W., Warden, Civil Defence Service 27/04/42
Self, V.R.C., Pte 5 Som (Bath City) Bn HG 26/04/42
Smith, L.H., Fireman, AFS (V) 27/04/42
Snook, K.E., Constable, Bath City Police 27/04/42
Woods, A.R., Pte 5 Som (Bath City) Bn HG 26/04/42
Woods, W.H., Warden, Civil Defence Service, 26/04/42

APPENDIX 3
BATH'S WAR DEAD

KILLED ON ACTIVE SERVICE 1939–45 – PART I

Below are listed the names of more than 500 men and women from Bath and District who died while serving in the British armed forces and Merchant Navy at home and overseas, or with the Civil Defence Services. The information has been obtained from a variety of sources that include the Bath city war memorial in Victoria Park, the Commonwealth War Graves Commission (CWGC) register of war dead, the Book of Remembrance held at Bath Abbey and at St John's, South Parade, and from various wartime issues of the *Bath & Wilts Chronicle and Herald*.

It is not a complete listing but to the best of the authors' knowledge it is the most definitive available at the time of publication. It does not include civilians killed during the Bath Blitz and in other bombing raids (see Appendix 1), or civilians who served with the Civil Defence Services (ARP, AFS, Police, Medical Services etc.) (see Appendix 2).

There are almost certainly omissions to this list, which in themselves are regrettable. These are attributable to incomplete records in the city as well as a number of CWGC records that do not list names and addresses of next-of-kin. Thus, in some cases only the surname, initials and branch of the services of an individual are recorded in the list that follows.

When the roll of names was compiled for the city's war memorial in 1951, dozens of names were inadvertently left off. Similarly, the Book of Remembrance in Bath Abbey and at St John's, South Parade, suffers from being an incomplete listing. However, these books have been added to on at least two occasions since they were deposited in the city's churches.

Some names on the war memorial are not included in the Book of Remembrance and vice versa. Others are not present at all, either in the book or on the memorial. Sixteen names that appear on the war memorial relate to service personnel who died after 15 August 1945 (VJ–Day) and are not included in this list because they fall outside the scope of this book.

The personal information recorded below is presented as follows: surname, initials, rank, (awards and decorations), unit and/or branch of services, ship or squadron, date of death (the latter is as listed in the CWGC register).

Abrahams, D., Pte 1 Bn KOYLI 04/02/44
Adams, A.A., AC1 RAFVR 17/06/40
Adams, C., L/Cpl 5 Bn Wilts Regt 08/03/45
Adams, F.N.V., L/Cook (S) RN,
    HMS Sultan 16/02/42
Adkins, F.H., Pte 2 Bn R Berks Regt 05/05/45
Allen, A.M., Pte 7 Bn Parachute Regt 24/03/45
Allen, D., Pte 2 Bn Som LI 22/09/44
Allen, D.R., Sgt RAFVR, 50 Sqn 29/07/44
Appleford, A.H.N., Sgt RAFVR,
    9 FTS 08/09/40
Archer, H.A., Stoker 1st Cl RN,
    HMS *Galatea* 14/12/41
Archer, V.H., Sgt RAF, 214 Sqn 23/05/43
Arthurs, S.A., Pte 2 Bn Glos Regt 10/05/40
Ash, E.P., Pte 308 Res MT Coy
    RASC 26/04/41
Ashley, C.H., F/S RAF, 19 OTU 24/09/40
Ashman, A.C., Sgt RAFVR, 214 Sqn 07/12/40
Ashman, S., Sgt (BEM) 4 Bn Som LI 10/07/44
Ashton, J.H., Lt 5 Bn Hants Regt 26/02/43
Aust, L.R., F/L (DFC, DFM) RAFVR,
    224 Sqn 07/06/44

Baatz, G.A.F., Gnr 71 Field Regt RA 03/01/44
Baker, A.J., Dvr 261 Field Pk Sqn RE 27/01/42
Baker, M.L., Spr 204 Field Coy RE 13/11/40
Bampfylde, H.W., Pte 6 Bn Green
    Howards 10/08/44
Barrett, K.S., Supply Asst RN,
    HMS *Bonaventure* 31/03/41
Bath, E.J.L., AC2 RAF
    (on HMS *Courageous*) 17/09/39
Batham, R.J., Sgt RAFVR, 15 Sqn 29/01/44
Barton, C., Pte Pioneer Corps 29/05/44
Beacham, E.N., Craftsman REME 30/09/44
Beaverstock, G.G., Gnr 5 Field
    Regt RA 29/11/42
Bethell, R.F., Pte 4 Bn Som LI 17/01/41
Bishop, C.E., Sgt 2/7 Middx Regt 24/02/44
Bishop, D.J., Pte Lt 7th Light Cavalry
    Regt, Indian Army 16/05/44
Bishop, J., AB RN, HMS Venetia 19/10/40
Bishop, W.H., Stoker 1st Cl RN,
    HMS *Kite* 21/08/44
Blackmore, A.N., L/Cpl 1 Bn
    R Sussex Regt 22/11/41
Bond, A.G., AB RN,

HMS *Prince* of Wales 10/12/41
Book, E, Pte 1 Bn R East Kent Regt 09/09/44
Booker, G.A., OS RN, HMS *Eclipse* 24/10/43
Botwood, H.A., Cpl 204 Fld Coy RE 13/01/41
Boughton, C.O., Maj 1 Bn E
    Yorks Regt 29/05/45
Bowler, J.A., Lt 7 Bn Parachute Regt 07/06/44
Bowyer, G.R., Pte 2 Bn Som LI 01/07/44
Boyd, N.W., 2/L R Norfolk Regt 18/11/42
Brain, C.E., Gnr 109 (7 Bn R Sussex
    Regt) Lt AA Regt 22/09/44
Brake, P.S., Cpl 2 Bn Som LI 22/09/44
Branch, L.A., Pte 1 Bn Loyal Regt 25/08/44
Bransgrove, A.E., F/O RAFVR,
    166 Sqn 30/07/43
Breakwell, R., F/O RAFVR, 61 Sqn 21/03/45
Brook, R.W., Sgt RAFVR 76 OTU 15/01/45
Brooker, A.A., Sgt RAFVR, 61 Sqn 13/09/40
Brooks, R.F., Sgt RAF, 210 Sqn 23/05/41
Brooksbank, D., Sgt RAFVR, 219 Sqn 06/12/41
Brown, A., Gnr 9 Coast Regt RA 13/02/42
Brown, J.D., Sgt 5 Bn DCLI 08/08/44
Brown, L.C.G., AC2 RAFVR 23/11/43
Brown, W.J., Pte 1 Bn R West
    Kent Regt 05/07/44
Bryant, L.B., Tpr, N Som Yeomanry 10/07/41
Bunston, P.R., Gnr 98 HAA Regt RA 07/10/42
Burgess, L.C., Dvr 261 (Airborne)
    Pk Sqn RE 08/06/45
Bush, K.S., F/O RAFVR, 105 Sqn 27/05/43
Butcher, T.A., Pte 5 Bn Dorset Regt 18/11/43

Caddey, E., Rfm 10 Bn Rifle Bde 21/02/45
Calley, S.J., Pte 4 Bn Som LI 20/01/40
Candy, A.R., 2/L Cyprus Regt 20/04/41
Carey, R.H., LAC RAFVR 2 FTS 06/11/41
Carson, C.E., Spr 54 Fld Coy RE 13/03/41
Carter, F.G., Spr 204 (Wessex)
    Fld Coy RE 12/09/42
Chambers, W.H., Pte 1 Bn
    Ox & Bucks LI 05/07/44
Champion, C.F.D., Stoker 1st Cl RN,
    HMS *Matabele* 17/01/42
Charles, P.S., F/L RAFVR, 33 Sqn 16/12/41

Chislett, K.E., P/O RAFVR, 51 Sqn 09/10/43
Clark, A.H., Sgt RAFVR, 101 Sqn 05/05/43
Clark, K.E.A., LAC RAFVR 06/07/45
Clark, R.A.W., PO Tel RN,
    HM S/M *Thames* 23/07/40
Clark, R.S., 4th Eng Off MN,
    SS *Empire Merlin* 25/08/40
Clark, W.H., AB RN,
    HMS *Avonvale* 29/01/43
Clarke, W., S/Sgt 2 Wing GPR 19/04/44
Clarke, A.H., Sgt RAFVR, 101 Sqn 05/05/43
Clarke, W.G., Spr 204 Fld Coy RE 08/08/44
Cleverley, F.T., Cpl 5 Bn Glos Regt 16/04/40
Coates, A.H., P/O RAFVR, 207 Sqn 17/07/43
Coates, G.F.A., 2/L General List 13/10/44
Coker, L., Maj Pioneer Corps 14/01/44
Coles, R.G., Sgt RAF, 166 Sqn 01/02/45
Coles, P.F.G., Pte 5 Som (Bath
    City) Bn HG 26/04/42
Combstock, W.H., Dvr 2 Line
    Maint Sect RCS 03/08/43
Comley, W.J., S/Sgt RASC 06/06/44
Commons, H., C/Stoker RN,
    HMS *Puckeridge* 13/12/41
Cook, J.R., Sgt 9 HAA Regt RA 28/11/42
Cook, J.W., Pte 4 Bn Som LI 06/08/44
Cook, R.G., Maj (MC Bar)
    4 Regt RHA 19/06/41
Cook, R.J., L/Sgt 61 AT Regt RA 30/10/42
Cook, T.E., Gnr 613 Maritime
    Regt RA 21/02/42
Cooke, E.J., Sgt RAFVR 15 OTU 18/09/43
Cope, R.C., LAC RAFVR 30 Sqn 14/06/41
Copsey, E.F.V., F/L RAF, 267 Sqn 22/10/42
Coombs, F.M., AB RN, HMS
    Caroline 15/04/41
Coombs, J.G., Pte 12 (Airborne)
Bn Devon Regt 25/03/44
Cossey, W.F., Pte 6 Bn S Wales
    Borderers 26/01/45
Costello, D.J., Spr 204 Fld Coy RE 13/11/40
Coulston, H.C., Capt 1 Bn King's
    Own R Regt 14/06/40
Cowley, D.J., Pte Som LI 26/01/44

Cox, G.E., OS RN, HMS *Glorious* 09/06/40
Croft, A.G., Gnr 373 Bty 55
    (W Som Yeo) Fld Regt RA 12/06/41
Crook, D.H.F., Pte 2 Bn S Wales
    Borderers 10/09/44
Cruse, W.A., Pte 4 Bn Som LI 13/10/42
Curran, J.A., WO2 RE 02/06/45
Curtis, H., Gnr 11 Coast Regt RA 12/09/44

Dachicour, C.I., L/Bdr 94 (Dorset &
    Hants Yeo) Fld Regt RA 30/05/45
Dagger, W.H., Cpl 1 Bn Som LI 27/01/44
Dansey, C.H., Lt 3/5 R Gurkha
    Rifles 15/03/44
Dann, W.E., Sgt RAF, 909/910
    Balloon Sqn 25/05/44
Darbishire, C.F., S/L RAF 11 Sqn 11/12/41
Davey, A.A., Sgt RAFVR, 50 Sqn 10/08/44
Davies, J., WO1 42 RTR
    (23 Bn London Regt) RAC 25/11/41
Davies, R., Pte 6 Bn S Wales
    Borderers 08/03/44
Davis, D.V., Sgt 4 Bn Som LI 30/06/44
Davis, G.W., Stoker 1st Cl RN,
    HMS *Eridge* 29/08/42
Dawe, R., Pte 2 Bn Som LI 28/09/44
Deadman, E.F., F/S RAFVR, 40 Sqn 15/04/44
Deas, J.H., P/O RAF, 26 Sqn 27/05/40
De Freitas, W.A.A., W/C (DFC)
    RAF, 70 Sqn 20/12/41
Denning, J.V., Apprentice M Navy,
    SS *Port Hunter* 11/07/42
Derrick, H.J., L/Bdr
    4 Maritime Regt RA 30/05/41
Derrick, L.J., Sgt RAF 12/09/42
Derrick, V.N., Tpr 3 King's Own
    Hussars RAC 20/06/44
Dimes, B.J., L/Cpl 5 Bn Dorset Regt 18/11/44
Dodd, W.J., Sgt 4 Bn Som LI 10/07/44
Dolling, K.H., Gdm
    5 Bn Coldstream Gds 29/06/44
Dottie, R.A., Pte W Yorks Regt 13/02/44
Dowding, G.E., OS RN,
    HMS *Gloucester* 22/05/41

Drewitt, M.A.F., Sgt RAF, 210 Sqn 02/09/40
Drummond, J.E., AB RN, HMS *Drake* 11/07/45
Durbin, A.C., Pte 5 Bn S Staffs Regt 16/07/44
Durnell, N.F., AB RN, HMS *Repulse* 10/12/41

Eacott, G., Stoker 1st Cl RN,
    HMS *Courageous* 17/09/39
Eades, W.W., CPO (Cook) S RN,
    HMS *Dorsetshire* 05/04/42
Eccles, G.S., PIO RAFVR, 99 Sqn 01/09141
Edie, F.M.W., Capt R Scots 25/10/44
Edridge, H.P., P/O RAF, 222 Sqn 30/10/40
Edwards, L.F., Lt RNR, HMS *Heron* 04/01/42
Elliott, F.R., Lt RNVR, HMS *Miranda* 21/08/44
Elliott, H.J.G., Capt 2 Bn Devon Regt 24/08/43
Elliott, S.J., L/Cpl 1 Bn Som LI 27/11/41
Elly, T.J., Pte 4 Bn Som LI 13/10/42
Emery, H.J., LAC RAF 12/09/42
Evans, I.T., Tpr 44 RTR RAC 08/11/43
Evans, R., Fus 1 Bn R Inniskilling
    Fusiliers 07/04/43
Evans, R.A.C., PO RN, HMS *Sultan* 15/03/42

Farmer, F.R., Spr 585 Corps Fld
    Pk Coy RA 07/01/43
Farnham, J., Pte 5 Bn Dorset Regt 10/07/44
Farrant, D.S., AB RN,
    HMS *Rawalpindi* 23/11/39
Featherstone, J.R., Gnr 226 Bty
    57 AT Regt RA 29/05/40
Fell, V.J., Dvr RASC 24/11/40
Fennell, A.E., PO RN,
    HM S/M *Unique* 23/10/42
Ferris, R.J., 9 Bn R Fusiliers 18/11/43
Filleul, P.R.S., F/L RAF, 214 Sqn 12/09/44
Fitzjohn, P.W., 2/L R Marines 29/08/40
Flaherty, M.J., Pte 2 Bn R Berks Regt 26/12/44
Fleming, W.A.J., Pte RAMC 09/09/40
Flower, G.E., Cpl 4 Bn Som LI 04/10/44
Forde, E.G., P/O RAFVR, 434 Sqn 16/02/44
Foreman, W.G., Pte 2 Bn Wilts Regt 10/06/44
Foreman, W.J., Stoker 1st Class RN,
    HMS *Calcutta* 01/06/41
Fouracre, S.C., Gnr 35 Sig Trg

Regt RA 19/03/41
Francis, L.J., P/O RAFVR, 53 Sqn 26/06/41
Frazer, J.D., volunteer (CdeG)
    Friends Ambulance Unit 23/11/44
Freeman, H., Stoker 1st Cl RN,
    HMS Dinosaur 07/11/44
French, M.J., F/O RAF, 210 Sqn 22/03/43
French, R.J., 2/L 5/
    18 Garhwal Rifles 21/01/42
Froud, R.F., L/Cpl 1 Bn
    Welsh Guards 10/09/44
Fry, A.F., F/S RAFVR, 434 Sqn 23/10/43
Fry, T.W., AB RN, HMS Dart 08/03/41

Gainey, A.E., LAC RAF 16/08/40
Gardner, B.G., OS RN,
    HMS Ganges 31/03/44
Gardner, R.J., L/Cpl 5 Bn
    R Sussex Regt 22/05/40
George, H.C., Pte 4 Bn Som LI 21/07/44
Gerrard, R.A., Maj (DSO)
    7 Fld Sqn RE 22/01/43
Gilbert, G., Pte 164 Fld Amb RAMC 29/05/40
Giles, S.W., Spr 204 Fld Coy RE 01/07/44
Gill, A.J.H., Pte 7 Bn Som LI 22/11/44
Glass, J.R., F/O RAFVR, 208 Sqn 27/10/44
Glen, R.G., PO (Cook) RN,
    HMS Abdiel 10/09/43
Goodfield, I.T., Spr 1238 Fld Coy RE 21/12/44
Gordon-Canning, C.J., L/Cdr RNVR
    SS St Lindsay 13/06/41
Gore, E.J.J., Pte RAMC 01/12/42
Goulding, A.H.R., Gnr 1 Regt RHA 10/05/41
Graham, L.J.A., P/O RAFVR, 12 Sqn 30/09/42
Grant, J.F., PO Stoker RN,
    HMS Charybdis 23/10/43
Grant, T.J., F/S RAFVR, 190 Sqn 22/02/45
Gray, C.L., L/Cpl RAOC 30/05/40
Gray, T., Sgt (VC) RAF, 12 Sqn 12/05/40
Green, A.F., Cpl 3 Parachute
    Sqn RE 22/06/44
Green, P.F, Cpl 5 Bn Black Watch 19/11/44
Greenham, L.J., CPO RN, HMS
    Glen Avon 02/09/44

Greenman, W.L., Cpl 2 Bn Som LI 03/01/44
Greenwood, D.H., Cpl
    5 Bn R Marines 08/12/41
Griffin, J.J, Sgt RAFVR, 61 Sqn 15/08/43
Gullick, G., Pte 4 Bn Som LI 22/11/40

Hancock, R.W.A., Sgt
    R Inniskilling Fusiliers 07/04/43
Harrill, E.C., P/O RAFVR, 100 Sqn 04/09/43
Hart, L.C., Pte 7 Bn Som LI 29/04/45
Harvey, L.I., Cpl 152 Regt
    (11 King's) RAC 28/06/45
Harvey, M.C., F/S RAF, 97 Sqn 08/08/41
Harwood, F., Gnr 454 Bty,
    68 (1 Rifle) Bn Mon Regt 04/01/42
Harwood, F., AC1 RAF, 107 Sqn 17/04/40
I.A. Harwood, Pte ATS 20/05/43
Hatherill, W.H., Marine, R Marines,
    HMS Hood 24/05/41
Hatherley, F.E., Marine,
    RM Group MNBD01 01/06/41
Hawkins, E.A.R., L/Bdr 4/2
    Maritime Regt RA 03/03/43
Hay, A., Sgt 3 Bn Scots Guards 30/07/44
Hayward, S.D., L/Cpl
    7 Bn Parachute Regt 06/06/44
Hayward, S.G., Tpr, 3 RTR, RAC 05/07/43
Hefferman, H.T., L/S RN,
    HMS Tynedale 12/12/43
Hellier, F., L/Cpl Beds & Herts Regt
Hillier, F.J., Pte, 21st Ind Coy,
    Parachute Regt 20/10/44
Herridge, R.J., Spr, 204 Fld Coy RE 06/10/44
Hewlett, R.O., LAC RAF 16/08/40
Hibberd, J.A., Pte 8 (HD) Bn, Som LI 08/11/41
Hill, E.H., WO2 Dorset Regt 06/10/44
Hills, R.J., Spr 279 Fld Coy RE 13/11/44
Hiscocks, R.W.A., Gnr 1
    8 HAA Regt RA 22/06/43
Hobbs, A.P.R., F/O RAFVR, 108 Sqn 13/07/44
Hobbs, F., Gnr
    7 Coast Guard Regt RA 03/07/43
Holley, A.C., L/Airman FAA
    HMS Daedalus 24/04/41

Holloway, R.P., Sgt Som LI 19/08/42
Holmes, E.W., Pte 4 Bn Som LI 11/07/44
Holvey, A.K., F/O RAFVR, 236 Sqn 17/01/45
Hooper, S.G., Spr 553 Fld Coy RE 17/04/41
Hopkins, R.H., PO Stoker RN,
    HMS *Grasshopper* 22/11/43
Hughes, H.R., F/S RAFVR, 357 Sqn 06/04/44
Hughes, R.W., Sgt RAF, 10 FIS 07/06/43
Hunt, F.J., Stoker 1st Cl RN,
    HMS *Gloucester* 22/05/41
Hurley, K.J., Pte R East Kent Regt 01/06/42
Hutchings, L.R., Pte 8 Bn Durham LI 09/08/44

Inchley, G.F., Sgt 131 Detail Issue Dept,
    RASC 10/04/44

Jago, P.E.O., P/O RAF, 39 Sqn 20/08/40
James, R.W., Lt Col 5 Bn Som LI 11/07/44
Jameson, H.G., 2/L R Marines 26/08/40
Jamieson, P.W., Sigmn 1
    22 Fld Regt RA, Sig Sec 01/06/42
Jardine, L.A., Sgt RAFVR, 408 Sqn 25/01/42
Jefferies, J., Sgt 2 Bn Devon Regt 31/07/43
Jefferies, S.H.T., Cpl RE (att. 6 W African Fld
  Coy, WA Fld Engs, RWAFF) 24/06/43
Jones, D.G., Master, M Navy,
    MV *Sutlej* 26/02/44
Jones, G.L.M., AC1 RAF 29/11/43
Jones, J., Spr RE
Jones., N.E., Cpl 204 Fld Coy RE 15/08/44
Jones, R.A.T., Spr 4 Fld Sqn RE 22/01/45
Jones, R.D.H., LAC RAFVR 23/03/44

Keedwell, J., Sgt RAFVR, 158 Sqn 04/04/43
Keeling, J.E., Stoker 1st Cl RN,
    HMS *Courageous* 17/09/39
Keeling, T.G., L/Cpl 3 Bn
    Grenadier Guards 18/03/43
Kelly, E.W., L/Airman RN,
    HMS *Furious* 09/12/43
Kelly, J., AB RN, HMS *Hood* 24/05/41
Kelson, V.R., Gnr 98 (Surrey & Sussex
    Yeo) Fld Regt RA 28/01/44
Kennedy, J.S., Sgt RAF, 104 Sqn 02/07/42

Kent, J.B.E., Lt 7 Bn Som LI 07/06/43
Kettlety, A.R., Pte 7 Worcs (Malvern)
    Bn, HG 07/03/43
King, C.P., Sgt RAFVR, 9 Sqn 26/06/43
Kite, H.W.J., Pte 2 Bn Devon Regt 13/06/40
Knee, J.W., Dvr RASC 18/06/43
Knight, F.G., AC1 RAFVR 12/02/42
Knight, F.S., Sgt RAFVR, 148 Sqn 16/08/44
Knight, K.A.T., Pte 10 Bn Durham LI 04/02/45

Lacey, L.F., Pte Som LI 15/09/42
Lander, C.M., W/C RAF Regiment 24/04/45
Lane, W.A., Capt 5 Som (Bath
    City) Bn HG 23/07/44
Langbridge, E.H., Pte 2 (Airborne)
    Bn Ox & Bucks LI 27/06/44
Lansdown, L.A., L/Cpl 4 Bn Som LI 29/05/44
Lansdown, T., Pte 2 Bn Hants Regt 12/09/44
Lavington, E.W., Sgt 4 Bn Som LI 06/08/44
Lawley, V., Stoker 1st Cl RN,
    HMS *Courageous* 17/09/39
Lee, M., Sgt RAFVR, 421 (Recce) Flt 31/12/40
Lee, W.E., L/Cpl 1 Bn
    R West Kent Regt 03/07/44
Legg, R.W., LS (DSM) RN,
    HMS *Firedrake* 17/12/42
Lewis, A.J., Dvr RASC 31/05/40
Lewis, A.P., Sgt 91 Fld Regt RA 28/11/40
Lewis, R.A.L., F/L (DFC) RAF, 39 Sqn, 29/07/41
Lewis, W.E.R., OS RN,
    HMS *Laforey* 30/03/44
Lidiard, W.A., Sgt 1 Bn Wilts Regt 14/02/44
Long, W.H., Pte 1 Bn Som LI 21/05/42
Lowe, R.A., Pte 2 Bn Welsh Regt 28/02/45
Lyon-Williams, C., Lt 5 RTR RAC 12/11/43
Lumber, W.G., Pte RAOC 03/08/43
Lundon, W.E., P/O RAFVR, 56 OTU 06/06/42

Machin, A.G.G., P/O RAFVR,
    252 Sqn 01/08/42
Maggs, E.W.F., Sgt
    1 Bn Grenadier Guards 01/06/40
Manns., W.R., L/Cpl 8 Bn
    Worcs Regt 02/02/40

Mara, N.D., F/L (DFC) RCAF,
　　433 Sqn 04/02/45
Marquiss, D.R., Lt 2 Bn Hants Regt 04/12/44
Marsh, A.G., LS (DSM) RN,
　　HMS *Jupiter* 27/02/42
Marsh, A.J., L/Cpl (MM) 2 Bn
　　R Inniskilling Fusiliers 19/01/44
Martin, C., AC1 RAFVR 06/03/43
Martin, C.H., L/Cdr (E) RN,
　　HMS *Hermes* 09/04/42
Martin, R.M.S., A/S/Lt RN,
　　HMS *Ark Royal* 27/11/40
Maslen, T.A., F/S RAF, 8 AACU 25/10/41
Matthews, E.M., F/S RAF, 87 Sqn 14/11/41
Matthews, S.G., O/Teleph RN,
　　HMS *Hood* 24/05/41
Mauger, A.C., Tpr 3 RTR RAC 13/10/44
Meddick, G.R., Craftsman REME 04/07/44
Miles, F.W., Sgt Military Provost
　　Staff Corps 30/03/44
Miller, H.V., F/O RAFVR, 207 Sqn 03/03/45
Miller, N.W.C., Sgt RAFVR, 10 Sqn 02/05/44
Minns, P.W., AB RN,
　　HMS *Courageous* 17/09/39
Minty, K.B., Sgt RAFVR, 21 Sqn 23/07/41
Mitchell, D., Tpr N Som Yeomanry 10/07/41
Mitchell, G.E., Sgt RE 31/12/42
Mole, D.H., Pte 2 Bn Som LI 07/04/44
Moody, C.L., F/O RAFVR, 354 Sqn 07/10/43
Moon, P.C., Maj 3/8 Punjab Regt 08/02/44
Morgan, C.G., Stoker 1st Cl RN,
　　HMS *Courageous* 17/09/39
Morris, R.G., Gnr 7 Med Regt RA 07/04/42
Morris, T.O., Spr 9 (Airborne)
　　Fld Coy RE 21/09/44
Mortimer, S.J., L/Cpl 6 Bn
　　York & Lancaster Regt 02/01/45
Mould, R., Pte 3 Bn Monmouthshire
　　Regt 03/04/45
Mulliss, W.C., Sgt RAFVR, 22 Sqn 06/04/41
Mumme, R.M., Sgt RAFVR, 51 Sqn 17/04/43
Mundy, A.R., Gnr 186 Bty
　　74 Lt AA Regt RA 29/08/42

Naile, R.S., Sgt RAFVR, 196 Sqn 04/07/43
Newman, F.C., Stoker 1st Cl RN,
　　HM S/M *Thunderbolt* 28/03/43
Nicholls, C.G., Pte 2 (Airborne)
　　Bn Ox & Bucks LI 24/03/45
Noad, R.H.J., Sgt RAFVR, 616 Sqn 11/08/42
Noad, V.R., Pte 10 Bn Gloucs Regt 15/02/45
Northam, W., AB RN, HMS *Hood* 24/05/41
Norvill, W.H., Pte 1/6 Bn
　　Queen's R Regt 03/10/42
Nudds, A.G.S., CERA RN,
　　HMS *Culver* 31/01/42

O'Brien, J.P., S/Sgt, Z Craft
　　Op Coy RE 06/11/44
Oatley, M.G., Tpr 1 Bn Northants
　　Yeomanry RAC 30/10/44
Oatley, R.C., Stoker 2nd Cl RN,
　　HMS *Mahratta* 25/02/44
Odey, B.A., Gdm 4 Bn
　　Coldstream Gds 15/04/45
Osborne, S.G.J., L/Cpl 10 Bn Som LI 21/12/40
Owen, B.J., PO Airman FAA,
　　HMS *Courageous* 17/09/39

Page, A.W.H., WO RAFVR,
　　103 Sqn 03/08/43
Palmer, G.F., AB RN, HMLC(T) 127 19/08/42
Parent, S., Pte Le Regiment de
　　Maisonneuve, RCIC 26/08/44
Parfitt, L.W., P/O RAFVR, 218 Sqn 16/07/41
Parker, B.F., Spr 275 Fld Coy RE 25/06/44
Parker, L.H., F/O RAFVR, 1654 CU 24/05/43
Parker, M.F., AC1 RAFVR 25/05/43
Parsons, R.C., Stoker 1st Cl RN,
　　HMS *Salsette* 11/03/43
Patch, R.W., Sgt RAFVR, 285 Sqn 07/11/43
Payne, R.K., L/Cpl 4 Bn Som LI 10/07/44
Pearson, D.C., Pte 5 Som (Bath
　　City) Bn HG 26/04/42
Pellier, R., Dvr RASC 03/09/41
Perrett, E.N., Pte 2 Bn Argyll
　　& Sutherland Highlanders 15/07/44
Phillips, G.C., Tpr 46 Bn RTR RAC 24/07/43

Phillips, L.H., L/Cpl 7 Bn
  Parachute Regt 06/06/44
Pocock, W.H., Pte 1 Bn Dorset Regt 02/08/43
Pope, S.J., Sgt RAF, 166 Sqn 03/12/43
Prescott, G.G., Sgt RAF, 210 Sqn 15/03/41
Price, F.W., CPO (Cook) RN,
  HMS *Anking* 04/03/42
Prior, L.J., LAC RAF 23/03/41
Pritchard, F.J., Dvr RASC 20/04/45
Pritchard, R., AB RN,
  HMS *Courageous* 17/09/39
Purnell, D., Stoker 1st Cl RN,
  HMLC(T) 317 06/06/44

Quinlan, H., Spr 204 Fld Coy RE 31/08/40
Quintin, C., L/Bdr 3 Bty
  2 Maritime Regt RA 13/01/42

Ralph, H.K.V., Dvr RCS 25/03/45
Ransome, F.J., L/Cook RN 14/12/40
Rawlings, W.J., Pte General
  Service Corps 18/07/45
Read, A.P., Sgt RAFVR, 12 OTU 25/06/42
Read, C.N., Constable, Liverpool
  City Police 13/03/41
Reid, D.H., F/L (DFC) RAFVR,
  57 Sqn 26/06/43
Rendle, R.C., P/O RAFVR, 9 Sqn 09/04/41
Rice, E.G., Supply Asst RN,
  HMS *Eclipse* 24/10/43
Rice, V.A., Sgt RAFVR, 29 OTU 25/04/43
Richards, R.J., Spr 9 Fld Sqn RE 06/09/42
Richardson, C., Asst Cook RN,
HMS *Lagan* 20/09/43
Riddle, G.H., AC1 RAFVR 18/09/44
Ring, R.J., Rifleman 1 Bn Rifle Bde 13/06/44
Ritchie, J.M.T., Capt 1 Bn
  Ox & Bucks LI 28/05/40
Robbins, G.T., Pte 5 Som (Bath
  City) Bn HG 31/10/42
Roberts, J.E., Cpl 4 Bn Som LI 29/07/44
Robinson, F.W., Cpl 5 Bn Wilts Regt 29/12/43
Robinson, O.J., Cadet, M Navy,
  MV *San Victorio* 16/05/42

Rodger, J., L/Sgt 2/7 Bn
  Queen's R Regt 28/10/43
Rogers, S.W.G., Pte Army
  Catering Corps 23/09/44
Rose, L.A., Pte 2 Bn
  Sherwood Foresters 24/04/43
Rose, P.C., AC1 RAFVR,
  att. 808 Sqn 26/06/42
Rose, R., OS RN, MTB 417 16/03/44
Russell, J., Pte 4 Bn Suffolk Regt 09/10/43
Ryall, G.H., Pte 10 Bn Highland LI 28/06/44
Ryan, B., Bo'sun MN,
  SS *Queen City* 28/09/40

Saunders, R.R., L/Cpl Essex Regt 15/04/45
Sawyer, W.C., Tpr 47 Ind Sqn,
  Recce Corps RAC 17/05/42
Scott, R., L/Cpl 10 Bn Durham LI 03/08/44
Self, S.E., Gnr 4 Searchlight Regt RA 06/04/42
Sellick, W.E.H., Cpl Som LI 31/03/45
Seward, H.S., Sgt RAFVR, 114 Sqn 15/02/41
Shellard, W.H., Gnr 12 Bty
  6 HAA Regt RA 01/03/42
Sherman, K.G., Sgt RAFVR, 9 FTS 07/10/39
Simmons, J.A., Cpl RAF, 218 MU 07/08/44
Simpkins, G.A.W., L/Sgt
  3 Bn Coldstream Guards 22/06/44
Simpson, B.L.J., AB RN,
  HMS *Inglefield* 25/02/44
Singer, F.V., Pte 10 Bn Durham LI 28/06/44
Skeet, A.J.R., Cpl 204 Fld Coy RE
  (16 Bomb Disp Coy) 28/04/42
Skelton, A.S.W., PO Steward RN,
  HMS *Stanley* 19/12/41
Skinner, G.E., Cpl RAF 07/05/41
Skinner, W., Cpl Army Catering Corps
Slip, A.R., Cpl 2 Bn Som LI 05/08/44
Sloan, R.W., P/O RAFVR 17/01/41
Smith, F.W., AB RN,
  HMS *Gloucester* 22/05/41
Smith, G.H.J., F/O RAFVR, 54 OTU 01/12/44
Smith, H.T., Pte 7 Bn Ox & Bucks LI 10/11/43
Smith, K.M., Sgt RAF, 111(C) OTU 21/04/45
Smith, R.L., F/O RAFVR, 192 Sqn 05/07/44

Smith, W.A., Pte 2 Bn Som LI 14/12/44
Smith, W.T., F/L RAFVR, 2 FIS 19/12/44
Southerton, W.A.C., AC RAF 01/10/39
Spear, W.J.C., CSM 47 RM Cdo 02/11/44
Spencer, F.N.S., Craftsman REME 03/08/45
Spurway, F.J., WO2 2 Bn Som LI 15/10/42
Starr, J.F., 2 (Airborne) Bn
    Ox & Bucks LI 09/06/44
Stiles, E.G., OS RN, HMS *Hermes* 09/04/42
Stirk, J., Gnr 205 HAA Regt RA 06/06/44
Stockbridge, E.G., PO Stoker RN,
    HMS *Legion* 26/03/42
Stott, H.J., Spr 4 Fld Sqn RE 29/03/45
Stride, D., Pte 7 Bn Som LI 04/07/44
Sutton, W.H., CYS RN, HMS *Sultan* 27/02/42
Swallow, M.C.H., Rfm 2 Bn
    London Irish Rifles 21/06/44
Swatton, S., AC1 RAFVR 05/07/41
Swatton, S.G., Sgt 2/5 Bn
    Queen's R Regt 21/02/44
Sweet, H.G., L/Cpl Corps
    Military Police 08/06/40
Sylvester, E.J.H., P/O (DFC) R Aux
    AF, 501 Sqn, 20/07/40

Tanner, F.J., Cpl RE 02/04/42
Tanner, W.J., Pte Pioneer Corps 17/06/40
Tanner, W.J., Sgt RAFVR, 57 Sqn 01/08/42
Tatchell, W.J., Tpr 50 RTR RAC 21/04/43
Tavener, R.W., WO2 12 Bn
    Devon Regt 20/12/40
Thomas, J.G.L., Cpl 261 (Airborne)
    Fld Pk Sqn RE 19/11/42
Thomas, P.C., F/L RAF, 240 Sqn 07/05/41
Thorne, A.E.J., P/O RAF, 55 OTU 09/05/41
Thompson, L.G., Pte 2 Bn Wilts Regt 11/07/43
Thornton, W.J., Pte 11 Bn Durham LI 27/06/44
Thurgar, P.F.H., Sgt RAF, 87 Sqn 12/02/40
Tiley, J., Gnr 12 Bty 6 HAA Regt RA 02/06/45
Toone, J.H., P/O (DFC, DFM)
    RAFVR, 29 Sqn 27/11/42
Truman, P.A., Sgt RAFVR, 59 Sqn 30/06/41
Tudgay, F.W., Sig RCS 24/05/41
Turner, W.H., WO2 3 Amb Car

Coy RASC 21/10/41
Tylee, R.C., Pte Dorset Regt 20/11/42

Underwood, G.H., Sgt RAOC 14/01/45

Vaughan, P.W., P/O RAF, 4 Sqn 13/05/40
Vaughan, W.Y., Cpl (BEM)
    4 Bomb Disposal Coy RE 05/02/45
Vernon, M.H.S., RSM 173 Fld
    Amb RAMC 17/06/43
S.H. Vian, Sister QAIMNS 16/10/41
Vowles, R.J., Pte 10 Bn Green
    Howards 25/07/41

Waite, M., L/Cpl 141 Regt
    (7 Buffs) RAC 23/10/44
Wakefield, C.G.R., MAA RN,
    HMS *Titania* 28/09/39
Wakefield, E.R., Capt General List 03/06/44
Wakefield, F.R., Gnr 87 HAA
    Regt RA 06/03/43
Waldron, C.C., AB RN, HMS *Itchen* 23/09/43
Wallis, M.H. St J., Marine, R Marines,
    HMS *Hood* 24/05/41
Walsh, W., Cpl 5 Som (Bath
    City) Bn HG 27/04/42
Walton, B., LAC RAF 14/08/40
Ware, C., Cpl 1 Bn Wilts Regt 19/02/44
Ward, G.H., Pte 1 Bn Dorset Regt 12/07/44
Warren, J.V., AC2 RAFVR,
    927 Balloon Sqn 30/01/41
Warren, W.M., Pte 9 Bn Som LI 24/11/43
Watkins, J.C., Pte 4 Bn Som LI 17/12/44
Watson, R., Gnr 72 Fld Regt RA 22/03/42
Watts, A.J., Gnr 99 (R Bucks Yeo)
    Fld Regt RA 22/06/44
Watts, K.A.W., Fusilier 1 Bn R Fusiliers 15/12/43
Weaver, E.C., S/Sgt Army
    Dental Corps 11/05/42
Weaver, P.S., F/L (DFC) RAF,
    56 Sqn 31/08/40
West, H.A., Cpl 4 Bn Som LI 13/07/44
West, S.H., F/O RAFVR, 100 Sqn 15/04/43
Westlake, J.M., AC2 RAF 26/06/40

Wetten, N.E., L/Steward RN,
  HMS *Arbutus* 05/02/42
Wheeler, R., Cpl RAFVR BSRU 07/11/44
Wheeler, T.E.F., Gnr RN, HMS
  Hood 24/05/41
Wheeler, W.E., LAC RAFVR BSRU 07/11/44
White, J.C., Storekeeper, M Navy,
  SS *Fabian* 28/08/42
White, R.E., 4 Bn Som LI 09/08/44
White, T.R., Pte 2 Bn Wilts Regt 08/08/43
Whittaker, J., Sgt RAF 458 Sqn 24/08/43
Wickham, D.T., Lt RN HM MTB 695 07/03/44
Wickham, F.E., Marine, R Marines 02/07/44
Wilbraham, R.K., Spr 280 Fld
  Coy RE 13/06/41
Wilcox, R.L., L/Airman FAA,
  HMS *Colossus* 16/05/45
Wilce, J.C.G., F/S RAF, 57 Sqn 06/01/44
Wilkey, E.T., Sig 4 Air Form Sigs,
  N Som Yeo 28/08/42
Wilkins, C.H., ERA 4th Cl RN,
  HMS *Hermes* 09/04/42
Wilkinson, J.D., Tpr 11 R Hussars 19/07/44
Wilkinson, T.I.S., Spr RE 31/01/43
Williams, C.P., F/S RAF, 103 Sqn 18/08/43
Wilmington, S.T., LAC RAFVR 27/11/43
Wilmot, A.J., Sgt RAFVR, 38 Sqn 05/06/44
Wilton, D.C., Sgt GPR AAC 25–27/09/44
Wiltshire, L.G., Sgt RAFVR 12/09/42
Windmill, A.R., Pte 2 Bn Som LI 22/11/44
Winn, J.T., L/Cdr RN, HMS
  Matabele 17/01/42
Winship, T.W.H., 5 Bn Northants
  Regt 16/06/44
Witcombe, E.J., Marine, R Marines,
  HMLC PL713 08/07/44
Wolfe, R., L/Sgt 4 Bn Som LI 10/07/44
Wood, F.G., Pte 5 Bn Dorset Regt 27/06/43
Wood, F.H., Cpl RASC 20/06/42
Wood, M.G., Sgt RAFVR, 166 Sqn 13/07/44
Wood, R.H.V., Lt Int Corps 08/09/43
Woods, C.L., AC1 RAFVR 05/07/41
Wright, A.P., Sgt 3 Cas Clearing
  Stn RAMC 31/05/40

Wyatt, A.P.S., Craftsman 6 Tk Bde
  Wksp REME 24/06/44
Wyatt, H., Cpl 2 Bn
  London Irish Rifles 05/04/44
Wyatt, N.E., AB RN, HMS *Mourne* 15/06/44

Yaxley, R.G., G/C (DSO, MC,
  DFC) RAF 117 Sqn 03/61/43
Yeates, G.T., Pte 1 Bn King's
  Shropshire LI 05/05/43
Young, D.A., Sgt RAFVR, 612 Sqn 27/03/42

Abbreviations

Rank – AB Able Seaman; AC Aircraftsman; AC1 Aircraftsman 1st Class; Capt Captain; CPO Chief Petty Officer; CYS Chief Yeoman of Signals; Cpl Corporal; CSM Company Sergeant Major; Dvr Driver; CERA Chief Engine Room Artificer; ERA Engine Room Artificer; F/L Flight Lieutenant; F/O Flying Officer; F/S Flight Sergeant; Gdm Guardsman; Gnr Gunner; G/C Group Captain; LAC Leading Aircraftsman; L/Bdr Lance Bombardier; L/Cdr Lieutenant Commander; L/Airman Leading Airman; L/Cpl Lance Corporal; LS Leading Seaman; L/Sgt Lance Sergeant; Lt Lieutenant; Lt Col Lieutenant Colonel; MAA Master at Arms; Maj Major; OS Ordinary Seaman; PO Petty Officer; P/O Pilot Officer; Pte Private; Rfm Rifleman; RSM Regimental Sergeant Major; Sgt Sergeant; Sig Signalman; Spr Sapper; S/Sgt Staff Sergeant; S/L Squadron Leader; W/C Wing Commander; WO Warrant Officer; WO2 Warrant Officer 2; 2/L 2nd Lieutenant.

Units – AFS Auxiliary Fire Service; ATS Auxiliary Territorial Service; Bn Battalion; Bty Battery; Cdo Commando; Coy Company; DCLI Duke of Cornwall's Light Infantry; Fld Field; HAA Heavy Anti-Aircraft (Bty); HG Home Guard; HMS His Majesty's Ship; HM S/M His Majesty's Submarine; LI Light Infantry; Lt Light; MT Motor Transport; OTU Operational Training Unit; QAIMNS Queen Alexandra's Imperial Military Nursing Service; R Aux AF Royal Auxiliary Air Force; Regt Regiment; RAC Royal Armoured Corps; RAF Royal Air Force; RAFVR Royal Air Force Volunteer Reserve; RAOC Royal Army Ordnance Corps; RASC Royal Army Service Corps; RCS Royal Corps of Signals; RE Royal Engineers; REME Royal Electrical & Mechanical Engineers; RHA Royal Horse Artillery; RN Royal Navy; RNR Royal Naval Reserve; RTR Royal Tank Regiment; Sqn Squadron; Yeo Yeomanry.

KILLED ON ACTIVE SERVICE 1939–45 – PART II

Here follows the names of 76 men and women from Bath and District, who died while serving in the armed forces or with the Civil Defence Services, and for whom no further information can be found.

Aldum, F., Barnett, A., Beale, G.A.F., Campbell, D.G., Clark, H., Clark, J., Combes, J., Cox, A.G., Cox, J.A., Curtis, A.J., Curtiss, J., Davies, J.D., Davis, N., Dias, P., Dixon, J., Fox, P., Giles, S.T., Glenn, G., Gregory, J.F., Grovers, R.J., Groves, J., Hall, H., Harwood, J., Hay, C.D., Hayward, W., Hooper, L., Howe, R.W.C., Hulley, C., Jeffreys, A.F., Mahony, J., Mitchell, C.R., Norman, V., Norman, W., O'Reilly, L.B., Osborne, R.J., Packer, F.W., Palmer, S.V., Parfitt, D.G.R., Pike, G.P., Porter, J.A.M., Price, H.G., Pullen, H., Rawlings, E.T., Rendle, P.C., Riddaway, R.A., Robinson, E.W., Rose, R., Ryan, B., Sales, W., Saunders, W.H., Scott, R., Simpson, B.L.J., Skinner, H., Sloan, R.W., Smith, C., Smith, C.F., Smith, H.T., Smith, R., Soloman, W.C., Stamper, A.P., Starr, W.J., Sutton, W.H., Swatton, L.V., Thomas, R.C., Thompson, J.T., Todd, G.R., Todd, L.V., Todd, T.F., Truman, A.E., Tyers, G.A., Wakefield, R., Watts, A.J., Whitaker, N., Williams, C.P., Williams, G., Williams, J.D.